Updating for Business

MAKING SENSE OF MARKETING

The Complete Open Learning Course

WORKBOOK 2

MARKET RESEARCH AND PRODUCT DEVELOPMENT

MAKING SENSE OF MARKETING
The Complete Open Learning Course comprises:

1. WHAT IS MARKETING? (0–333–51112–3)
2. MARKET RESEARCH AND PRODUCT DEVELOPMENT (0–333–49838–0)
3. DETERMINING THE MARKETING MIX (0–333–49839–9)
4. ORGANISING AND PLANNING FOR MARKETING SUCCESS (0–333–49840–2)
THE BOXED SET (0–333–49837–2)

Also available from Open BTEC/Macmillan in 'Updating for Business':

COMPUTER STUDIES MS BASIC/GW BASIC VERSION (0–333–47144–X)
IMPLEMENTING SMALL BUSINESS COMPUTER SYSTEMS (0–333–44215–6)
INFORMATION TECHNOLOGY FOR MANAGERS (0–333–42937–0)
MANAGEMENT OF WORD PROCESSING (0–333–42965–6)

WORKING WITH PEOPLE (0–333–44204–0)
TRAINING AND COACHING SKILLS (0–333–42581–2)
MANAGING THE OFFICE (0–333–42562–6)
IMPROVE YOUR FINANCIAL DECISION MAKING (0–333–42952–4)

MAKING SENSE OF INFORMATION TECHNOLOGY (0–333–48537–8)
MAKING SENSE OF MARKETING WORKBOOK (0–333–42826–9)

Updating for Business

MAKING SENSE OF MARKETING
The Complete Open Learning Course

WORKBOOK 2

MARKET RESEARCH AND PRODUCT DEVELOPMENT

Peter Davies and David Pardey
The Further Education Staff College

Open
BTEC
MACMILLAN

First published 1990

Published by
MACMILLAN EDUCATION LTD
Houndmills, Basingstoke, Hampshire RG21 2XS
and London
Companies and representatives
throughout the world

British Library Cataloguing in Publication Data
Davies, Peter, 1947–
Making sense of marketing.
Workbook 2, Market research and product development
1. Marketing
I. Title II. Pardey, David
658.8
ISBN 0–333–49838–0

The complete Open Learning Course boxed set: 0–333–49837–2

Printed and bound in Great Britain by
Butler & Tanner Ltd, Frome and London

Contents

Acknowledgements

The publishers would like to thank the following for permission to use illustrative material:

Allan Waddell of American Express Europe Ltd; Donald Osborne of Donald Osborne Research Ltd and Sarah Baker of the Association of British Travel Agents for the ABTA study materials; Eileen Jay formerly of International Distillers and Vintners (UK) Ltd for her help on IDV case studies; Brian Godfrey and Margaret Roy of Roys of Wroxham Ltd for their case studies; Keith Davies of Midland Bank plc for the reproduction of the Orchard brochure; Janet Mayhew of JICNARS for the JICNARS National Readership Survey January 1989 classification page; Philip Mitchell of British Market Research Bureau for the Choices cross-tabulation and the housewives' version of the National Survey of Buying; Andrew Manly of Research Services Ltd for *SAGACITY A Special Analysis of JICNARS NRS 1980 Data undertaken by Research Services Limited*; Joanne Hindle of the Market Research Society for *Basic Principles* from the MRS Code of Conduct; Michael Watson of the Harris Research Centre, for the *Young Persons Omnibus*; David Piper of CACI Ltd for the ACORN profile of Great Britain; The Controller of Her Majesty's Stationery Office for 'Journey purpose' from *Social Trends* **18**, 1988.

Thanks also to Beryl Brett for her hard work in word processing Workbook 2.

Introductory Notes

This is the second of four open learning workbooks which make up the course *Making Sense of Marketing*. They have been written to support the BTEC Continuing Education unit *Making Sense of Marketing*, and, together with Tutor Assignments, make up a course of 60–90 hours of study. Successful completion of the course through a BTEC-approved centre can lead to the award of a BTEC Continuing Education Certificate.

A note about open learning

Open learning is a way of studying which allows you, the student, to plan and control your own learning programme to fit in with the other demands on your time – job, home, family and leisure activities. You choose where and when you want to work – the only limitations being the need to attend group study sessions, and submit items for assessment.

When you signed on for the course, your learning centre allocated a tutor, who is there to guide you through your study, and to make assessments which lead to the formal BTEC qualification.

Your tutor is there to provide support if you need it – to help sort out any practical difficulties you may encounter, to lend an ear if you have any problems with the learning itself, and to provide you with feedback on certain pieces of work which you will submit at various stages throughout the course.

What the course aims to do

Open BTEC courses are all about improving the skills you need to be more effective in your job – to update where necessary, perhaps to refresh your knowledge, or to acquire new skills which will enable you to develop your role at work. Above all, they aim to encourage you to apply what you are learning to your own particular place of work, and to the strengths, weaknesses, problems and people that you face in your everyday life at work.

Making Sense of Marketing aims to encourage you to 'think marketing', by:

● developing an understanding of marketing as an organisational philosophy, both for profit and non-profit organisations;
● developing an understanding of the roles of people involved in marketing;
● developing practical skills which you will be able to use in your current and future jobs.

The learning in the course is based on the achievement of the following six objectives:

● to use market research as a basis for marketing decisions;
● to make market-oriented product decisions;
● to assess the distribution strategy of a specific organisation or industry;
● to devise an effective marketing communications plan for a specific organisation;
● to contribute to the design of a marketing plan for a specific organisation.

You will see that these objectives are worded so as to emphasise the practical nature of the course – the focus on what you will actually be able to *do* when you have completed it. The course materials supply the basics, although much of the coursework and assignments will be set in the context of your own organisation, or one you know well.

The course materials

The course materials consist of four workbooks:

Book 1: What is Marketing?
Book 2: Market Research and Product Development
Book 3: Determining the Marketing Mix
Book 4: Organising and Planning for Marketing Success

The workbooks are exactly what their name suggests – books to work in. Each workbook contains spaces for you to answer the Activities – although you may need to overflow onto extra paper for some of them! You will then have a complete record of what you have learned when you have completed the course.

The Activities come in several different forms, each of which has a specific job to do in helping you learn:

Reflective activities, for which the symbol ⟩⟨ is used. These are intended to get you thinking about something which you have just read, to reflect on what has been said, perhaps jot down some notes, and get it clear in your mind before moving on to the next idea. There are usually no 'answers' to this type of activity – just the development of the idea in the text that follows.

Written activities, for which the symbol ✎ is used. These activities ask you to jot down some answers – usually nothing more than brief notes are required, although occasionally you will be asked to write something a little more meaty. 'Answers' to these are given sometimes in the text which follows, and sometimes at the back of the workbook. You will see that there are seldom 'right' or 'wrong' answers to these activities – just some guidelines against which to compare your thoughts.

Practical activities, shown by the symbol ✳ . These are usually mini-projects, which will help you to apply what you are learning, or do some research which will help to prepare the ground for tutor assignments. You will often be free to select the subject of these activities, and your tutor will always be available to help if you have any difficulty in selecting or carrying them out.

Progress tests, which appear at the end of Chapters 2, 3 and 4. These are designed to help you monitor your own progress in a more formal way – to give you a chance to check that you have understood a piece of work before moving on to the next chapter. If you are not happy with your work at these points, you can always contact your tutor to discuss any problems.

Planning your time

This course is designed to provide you with between 60 and 90 hours of study. This includes the time it takes to work through the workbooks, plus time allocated for you to complete any assignments which your tutor sets. You may take more or less time and still complete the course successfully.

At the beginning of the course, you should discuss with your tutor a timetable for completion of assignments – these dates often have to be fixed to coincide with group discussion sessions at your study centre. How you organise your time to meet these dates is entirely up to you. This is one of the benefits of open learning – you set your own deadlines and try to keep to them. You can even give yourself rewards for achieving your targets, or penalties for missing them!

Most students find that it helps to be systematic about where and when they work, setting aside a specific time each day or week to study – perhaps during their lunch hour, or between nine and ten each evening. Planning to work in this way encourages you to stick to your study plan, and helps to avoid distractions.

Use the timetable outline given below to plan your work for this Workbook. Add in any dates for assignment work that you have agreed with your tutor, then plan the rest of your time so that you can complete the work by an agreed date. An approximate study time is given for each chapter of the Workbook. You may be able to complete some chapters in a single session – others you may prefer to split between two sessions over a couple of days.

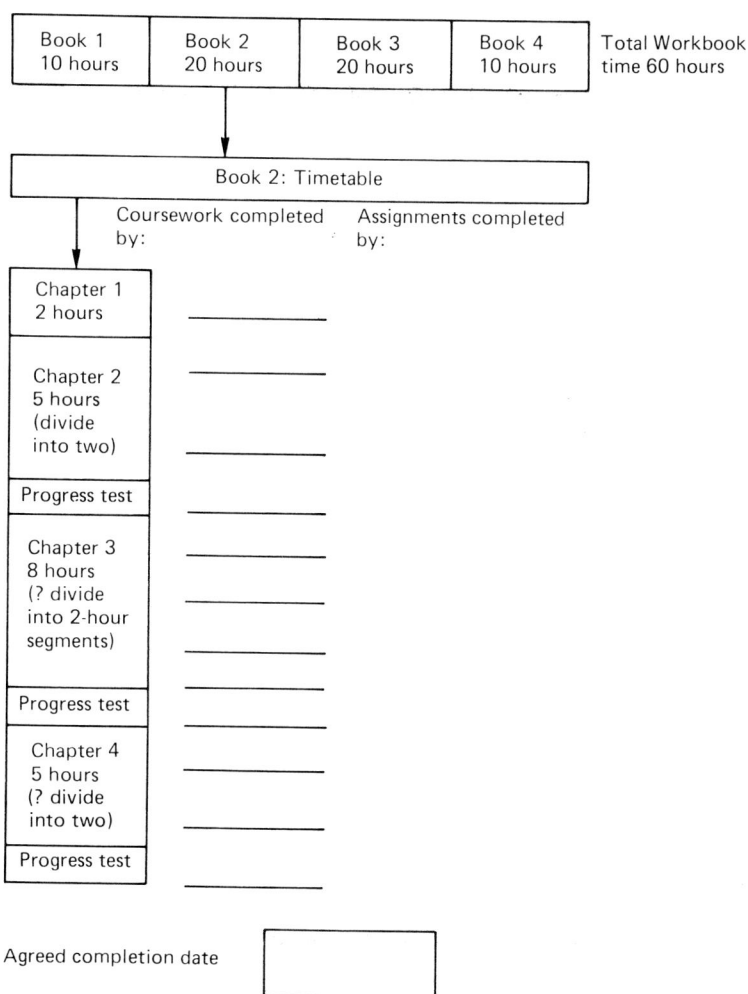

Book 1 10 hours	Book 2 20 hours	Book 3 20 hours	Book 4 10 hours	Total Workbook time 60 hours

Book 2: Timetable

	Coursework completed by:	Assignments completed by:
Chapter 1 2 hours	_____	
Chapter 2 5 hours (divide into two)	_____	
Progress test	_____	
Chapter 3 8 hours (? divide into 2-hour segments)	_____	
	_____	
Progress test	_____	
Chapter 4 5 hours (? divide into two)	_____	
Progress test	_____	

Agreed completion date ☐

The course contents

The contents of the four workbooks are listed below to give you an overview of the work involved. Throughout the course, case studies are used to give illustrations of marketing in practice. The case studies have been chosen to give examples from as wide a spectrum of types of organisation as possible.

A note for tutors

The tutor plays a vital role in helping the student study effectively by open learning. The role is essentially a supportive one – helping the student to plan and organise their time and providing feedback on certain pieces of work leading up to the final assessment. Throughout the course you should expect and encourage students to keep you informed of their progress, and investigate any prolonged silences.

We suggest that wherever possible you meet the student at the beginning of the course to agree a study timetable, setting up a 'contract' of significant dates at the outset.

Assessment items

Your choice of assessment items will depend on your own situation and that of your students – their number, work experience and so on. You will probably want to write your own assessment materials to meet these specific needs – indeed, market research lends itself to practical assessment work. Students can be asked to select a product or products (preferably connected with their own work), and to devise a market research project as they work through the Workbook.

If you choose to adopt this approach, make sure that students are clear as to what they will be doing before they start the Workbook, and agree dates to review their project work at suitable points in the learning sequence. For example, having decided on the product to be researched at the start of this part of the course, you could review progress (and assess at each stage if you consider it appropriate) at the following points:

After Chapter 2: an outline of the main questions about the current market (or potential market if it is a new product) to be answered, and an interim report on findings so far using desk research.

After Chapter 3: a plan for a market research project (which students may or may not be able to carry out during their work on the course).

Alternatively, you may prefer to leave assessment until after the Workbook has been completed, to identify a new product and devise a market research project from scratch at that stage.

Objectives

After working through this Workbook, you will be able to:
- define the term market research, and describe the contribution market research can make to wider marketing activities;

- explain the concept of a Market Information System and the role of market research in such a system;

- identify the market information which can be obtained from manual and electronic record systems;

- explain why statistical and other mathematical models are important in forecasting market demand;

- describe the main sources of market data available to desk researchers;

- describe the main steps involved in designing and using a market research project;

- explain the importance of questionnaire design and sampling strategy;

- recognise the main methods of customer classification;

- describe the contribution which omnibus surveys can make to a market research strategy;

- explain how new products are developed and launched;

- use various techniques for identifying new market opportunities and for analysing strengths and weaknesses in a product range;

- explain the use of test markets, and identify the features of a market which make it suitable for testing new products.

1 Researching the Market

After working through this chapter you will be able to define the term market research and describe the contribution market research can make to the wider marketing activities. You will also be able to explain the concept of a Market Information System and the role of market research in such a system.

Introduction

In working through the first workbook in this series you met many of the basic principles of marketing. In particular you saw how important it is to look at things from the customer's point of view. You also discovered something about the role marketing has to play in both public and private sector organisations, with very different objectives.

Those organisations which only consider what it is possible to make or supply to the market will never be as successful as organisations which consider the views of their customers.

ACTIVITY 1

>←

1 min

Two expressions are used to describe these different approaches. Can you recall them?

The organisation which looks at itself from the customer's point of view is 'market orientated' or 'market centred'; the one which doesn't is 'product orientated' or 'product centred'. This distinction is very relevant to the work we will be doing in this workbook, since we will be concentrating on how to discover the customer's point of view, and seeing how this can influence the product, and the way it is marketed. In other words, being market centred!

ACTIVITY 2

2 mins

In the first workbook, you also learnt about the marketing mix, *often described using the 'four Ps'; can you remember what they stand for?*

P _____
P _____
P _____
P _____

The marketing mix is the shorthand way of describing the main areas in which marketing can have an effect. It can shape what is on offer (the product), how it is presented and sold (promotion), how much it costs (price) and where it is available (place).

We are confident that you identified the 'four Ps' correctly. They may seem fairly obvious, but they sum up what marketing is all about. In particular it is worth emphasising that the product itself is also a marketing responsibility. In this book we shall be concentrating on how we can gather information about the customer's point of view and how that information can be used to develop new products to meet those customers' needs.

What is market research?

Have any of these things ever happened to you?

- Someone stops you in the street, or visits you at home or telephones you, to interview you.
- You find a questionnaire in a magazine you read which asks you about yourself, and which you are then asked to post to the publishers.
- You buy a new product and find a reply-paid card inside the box which asks you to register your ownership (and also asks where you got the product and other questions about you).
- You have to fill in a lengthy questionnaire about yourself, your income, your home and family, when applying for credit or a loan.

'I thought he was a bit offhand when you asked if he preferred his apples red or green.'

You have probably experienced at least one of these. Each one is an example of a technique of market research. In this chapter you will be introduced to the different ways of researching the market, and will learn how to be sure about precisely what sort of information you are collecting.

Look at the four examples of market research techniques we started with. Write down briefly why you think an organisation would need to use such techniques.

Compare your ideas with ours below.

2 mins

Most organisations these days don't know their customers in the way that small shopkeepers know their regular, local customers. If they are to be market-centred such organisations have to find out the customer's point of view and this means going to the customers and asking them. All the techniques we have listed can help in this process. This is sometimes the sole purpose of the exercise (as in the first two examples). Sometimes information is obtained during another transaction (as with the other two).

'. . .the way that small shopkeepers know their regular, local customers.'

Our first case study illustrates the problem experienced by large organisations in obtaining information about their customers' point of view.

●●●

CASE STUDY: Association of British Travel Agents (ABTA)

In the latter half of 1988 ABTA was concerned to counter adverse comments made in the press about travel agents and package holiday operators. These criticisms were generally the result of problems experienced by a small minority of holidaymakers, yet they gained great prominence despite that fact that the majority of holidays were trouble-free.

However, ABTA members (the travel agents) found it difficult to obtain proper feedback from their customers, since they were unlikely to see them again after their holidays, unless they booked for another package the following year. Even if they did make a repeat booking, seeing a customer once or twice a year is not frequent enough to build up the sort of relationship which ensures good market information about how the customers perceived their holidays, and what they thought of the service provided by travel agents. Getting feedback and acting on it used to be easy when travel agents sold tailor-made packages to suit the needs of individual clients. Nowadays, however, most customers buy a

standard package holiday supplied by a tour company. The agent is the retailer and has no direct influence over the make-up of the package, other than by deciding whether or not to 'stock' it, by offering it through the agency. The tour company, in turn, is attempting to gain economies of scale, through offering a standardized package, in order to ensure prices which are cheap enough to sell to a mass market.

Because of the difficulties in getting feedback from customers buying package holidays ABTA decided to conduct some market research to provide objective data on customers' experiences and perceptions of the products they had purchased. The market research they conducted provides a substitute for the personal relationships and individual feedback of an earlier age.

Later in this workbook we will be looking at some of the techniques used by ABTA in their research project.

●●●

But market research isn't only used to find out about customers' attitudes to the product; it can also be used to provide information about other aspects of an organisation's marketing activity. For example it can help to solve a problem voiced many years ago by Viscount Leverhulme, head of Lever Bros, now part of the giant multinational Unilever:

> 'Half the money I spend on advertising is wasted and the trouble is, I don't know which half.'

ACTIVITY 4

How do you think an organisation could go about solving the problem described by Viscount Leverhulme? Stop reading and make a few notes on how you would approach this difficulty. Compare your ideas with those outlined below.

2 mins

One way of finding out which advertising was effective could be to ask people which advertising for a particular product they have actually seen, and assess their reactions to it (ideally such reactions would be discovered in a 'test' before the proposed advertising is widely used). Alternatively particular parts of an advertising campaign could be stopped, in turn, to find out whether sales are affected by their inclusion or exclusion. Checking on the effects of advertising campaigns is another form of market research.

Some marketing textbooks make distinctions between research into *markets* (i.e. the customers), and research into *marketing*, which includes research into advertising. The terms 'market research' and 'marketing research' are used to distinguish between these different emphases. These terms are not always used in the same way though, so you may also find the term 'marketing research' used in American textbooks, and in some British ones, as an all-embracing term for both activities.

We shall describe all such research as 'market research', but you should remember that used in this way, the term can include researching into marketing activities as well as reactions to the product.

We can now offer you a definition of market research. Market research is the process by which an organisation investigates its market (or potential market) to assess reaction to actual (or potential) products, promotion and distribution strategies and prices.

ACTIVITY

5

→←

1 min

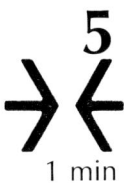

There are a number of elements of the marketing mix in this definition. How many can you find?

Our definition of market research includes *all* aspects of the marketing mix – product, promotion, price and place. The definition also suggests that market research is not just concerned with what is *currently* happening but also with what *might be* happening in the future.

What the definition doesn't include is a statement about *how* market researchers set about their work. There is no mention of surveys and questionnaires, for example. In Chapter 3 we will see that these are important parts of market research, but before that we will discover that there is a lot more to market research than just that.

Market Information Systems

Market research is one (very important) way of gathering and analysing information about the market. However, the *raw data* on the market – facts and figures about customers, their buying habits, attitudes etc – can also be collected in a number of other ways. The sifting of this raw data, organising it into a form that can be easily understood, converts it into useful *information*. In this section, we shall be looking at the main techniques for gathering data. We shall also see how useful marketing information can be derived from it.

A general term to describe the range of techniques for gathering and analysing data about the market is a Market Information System (or MIS). We have already suggested that market research is one important part of such a system, but various other sources of information about the market contribute to our understanding of it.

ACTIVITY

6

10 mins

You work in the Marketing department of a large organisation. You have been asked to find out useful information about the size of the market and about the current customers. Unfortunately, there isn't time to organise a formal survey of actual or potential customers. Where do you think you might be able to find such information, either inside or outside the organisation? Write a paragraph or two explaining how you would go about the task.

Compare your notes with the text which follows.

Market research activities involving surveys and questionnaires can obviously provide a lot of information, but they are not the only source of useful facts about the market. There are many existing published sources of relevant information, such as Government publications, yearbooks, directories, etc. These are all part of the range of sources which are available for *desk research*, a part of MIS which can be used to support or replace the *survey-based* methods of commissioned market research. You might also have spotted the importance of some of the information an organisation collects as part of its normal activities: sales figures, customer details, reports by sales staff, etc. These *internal marketing records* are a major part of an organisation's MIS.

Finally it is possible for an organisation to engage in various forms of statistical analysis of data to tell it about the market place. These *mathematical models* can be of varying degrees of sophistication and they enable an organisation to ask 'what if' type questions, which are answered partly on the basis of prior experience, which is built into the model. The models used rely on statistical theories and ideas from a branch of economics called econometrics.

The way in which organisations collect and use information from these sources determines how well they know (and understand) their customers. An adequate MIS should tell them at least who their customers are and give them some idea about who is not a customer and why!

Figure 1 on page 18 illustrates the four different elements of an MIS. The arrows show how the different sources of information support each other. If you look at how an organisation actually works, it isn't always as easy to separate the elements of an MIS from each other so neatly as in the diagram! In this chapter and the two which follow we will be looking at each of these elements in more detail.

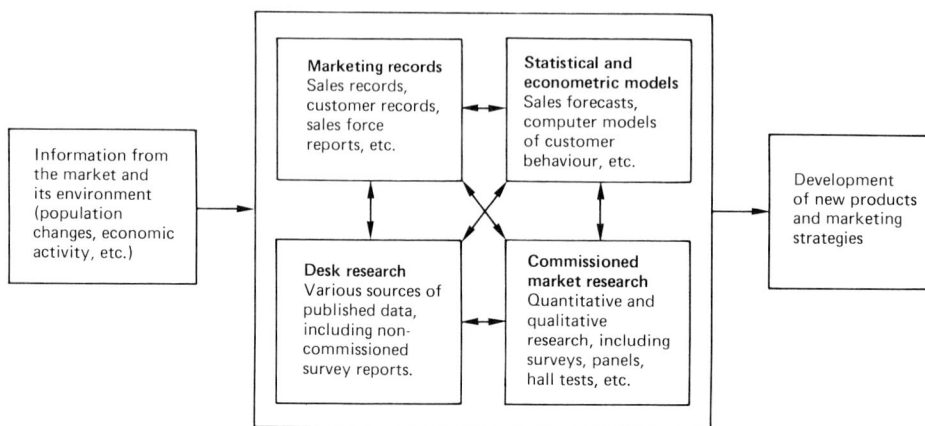

Adapted from 'Strategic Marketing for Educational Institutions' Kotler & Fox (Prentice-Hall: 1985)

Figure 1 A Market Information System

●●●

CASE STUDY: Metrocentre

The Metrocentre is the United Kingdom's largest out-of-town retail development, near Gateshead, Tyne and Wear. It has a complete range of shops, from traders selling goods from a 'barrow', to major department stores and a supermarket. The whole centre is enclosed in a single two-storey building which also has a leisure complex and a funfair.

Metrocentre operates a Market Information System which involves both the constant monitoring of customers (counting vehicle movements, collecting sales figures, etc.,) and *ad hoc* research (using some of the market research techniques we shall be exploring later). This enables it to identify information of value to all its retail operators, and to the centre itself in its marketing activities.

For example, Metrocentre's MIS supplies the information that during 1988 it was visited by an average of 308,000 people per week, peaking at 450,000 in the week before Christmas. Each visitor on average stayed 2.8 hours and spent £59; 24 per cent travelled from outside the North-East, and about 75 per

cent travelled by car. The age, sex and social class profile of the visitors is shown in the table below.

Mathematical modelling using sample vehicle counts enabled projections of the flow of vehicles to the site to estimate that 6.4 million vehicles visited the Metrocentre during 1988, with a peak of 723,000 during December alone.

To attract the 16 million visitors a year in 1988 Metrocentre spent £900,000 on marketing, a cost of 5.6p per visitor or less than 0.1 per cent of the average spend per visitor.

This information, which came from survey-based market research, market records and mathematical models, gives a detailed picture of the customers of Metrocentre. By comparing this with information about the total population in the catchment areas and their shopping habits using desk research, a complete picture of the market – who uses Metrocentre, and who doesn't – can be obtained.

Age		Sex (adult 16+)		Social Class	
Under 16	20%	Male	39%	AB	22%
16–24	18%	Female	61%	C1	31%
25–29	13%			C2	30%
30–39	19%			DE	17%
40–49	14%				
50–59	9%				
60+	6%				

●●●

ACTIVITY

7

5–10 mins

Figure 22 on page 73 shows the proportions of the United Kingdom population in the same social class classification system as that used to analyse Metrocentre's customers. (Note that AB and DE are simple ways of describing combined groups of A and B, and D and E.)

Knowing that the adult population of the United Kingdom is split 48.7 per cent male and 51.3 per cent female, what conclusions would you draw about the customers who come to Metrocentre from the information in the case study?

Compare your answer with the one on page 128.

ACTIVITY

8

5 mins

Below is a copy of Figure 1, but with all the boxes empty, and below it is a list of six descriptions of items of marketing information or market research activity, labelled A to F. Write in each of the empty boxes in Figure 2 the letter corresponding to the description which you think is appropriate to that element of the market information system.

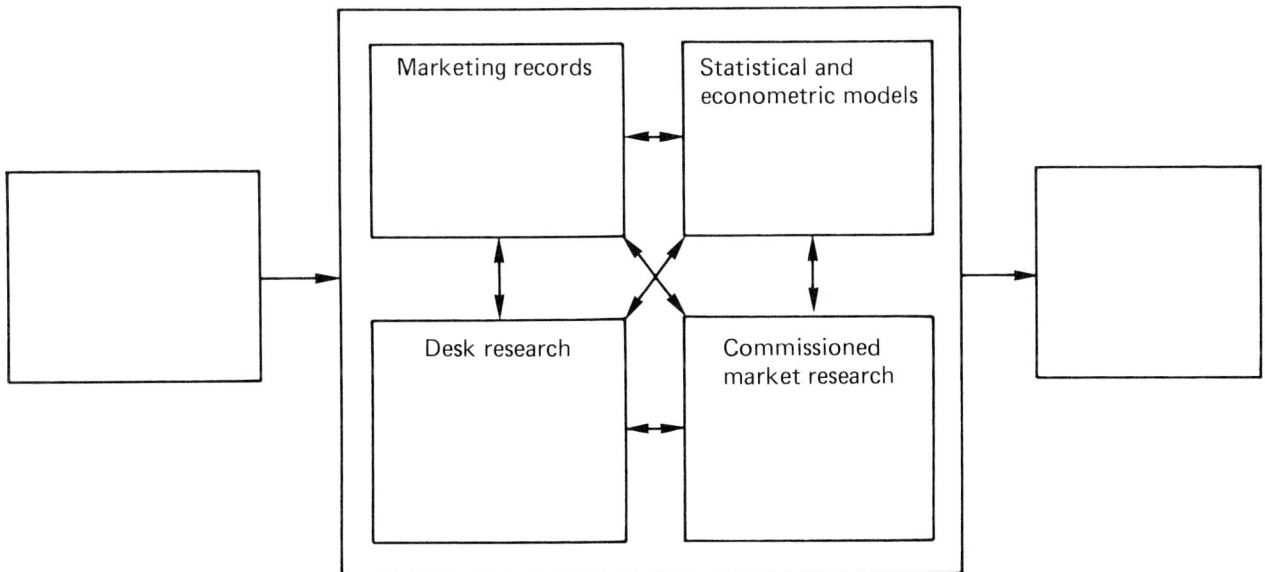

Figure 2

A. A publication called the Family Expenditure Survey *is available in most libraries and gives details of the consumption patterns of average families.*

B. *Every week sales representatives in a company submit a report on their customer visits that week.*

19

C. In 1988 the Association of British Travel Agents arranged for a survey of 924 people on their attitudes to travel agencies.
D. Between 1986 and 1994 the number of 16 year-olds in the United Kingdom will fall by over 25 per cent.
E. Shortly after the success of Cadbury's 'Wispa', Rowntrees redesigned and relaunched their 'Aero' chocolate bar.
F. A 'weighted moving average' is a statistical technique for identifying the pattern of sales by removing the more erratic fluctuations.

Compare your answers with the ones on page 128.

What is marketing information?

Information is often described as the most important asset of modern industry. The 'information technology' revolution has enabled us to collect, store and analyse far more data than ever before – sometimes far more than we might ever want! But what sort of information is it and how does it vary? In this section we shall look at the nature of the information about markets which can be collected, and give you an insight into how it can be used.

The most important distinction to make is between *number-based data* and *descriptive data* which is based on words rather than numbers.

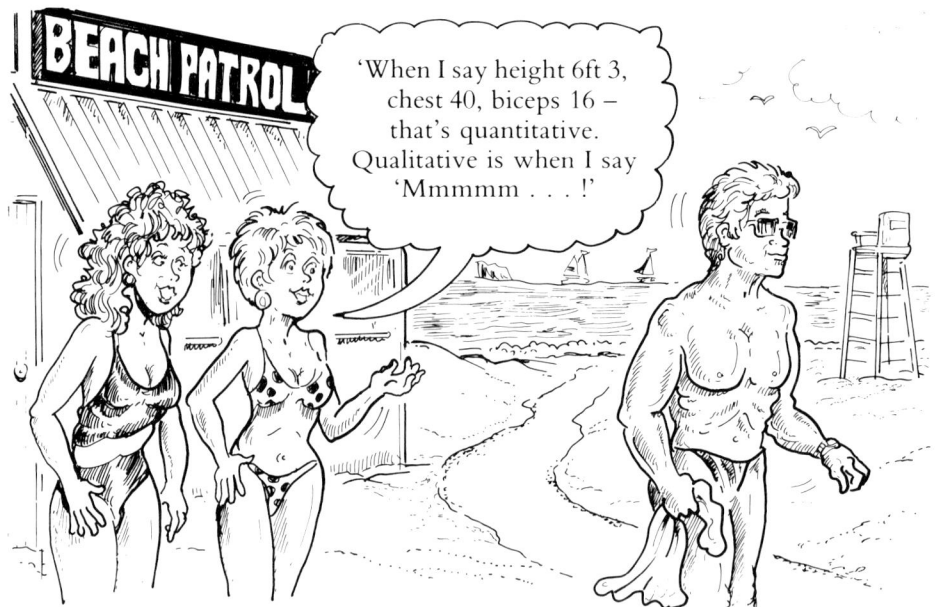

'When I say height 6ft 3, chest 40, biceps 16 – that's quantitative. Qualitative is when I say 'Mmmmm . . . !'

Qualitative and quantitative information

Numerical information is usually described as *quantitative*. It has certain advantages since it can be subjected to various mathematical or statistical techniques which allow very accurate deductions to be made. Descriptive or non-numerical information is known as *qualitative*. You can see from the next Activity some of the ways in which quantitative information can be used.

On Monday a salesman makes 12 visits and obtains 6 orders, on Tuesday he makes 14 visits and gets 7 orders, on Wednesday 10 visits produce 5 orders, on Thursday he makes 13 visits, getting 6 orders and on Friday 11 visits also produces 6 orders.

Calculate:
a) how many visits he makes in the week;
b) how many orders he obtains;
c) his average number of visits and of orders per day;
d) how many visits he makes on average to obtain one order.

If a typical salesman in the organisation has to make three visits to get one order, is this salesman better or worse than the others?

You will find the answers to the calculations on page 128.

This Activity is a very simple illustration of the sort of analysis it is possible to undertake using quantitative data. In this case the information we have acquired tells us something about the effectiveness of one salesman compared with his colleagues in terms of number of orders per visit.

Of course we didn't look at the value of orders or the area in which this individual operates. It may be that he gets a lot of low value orders. On the other hand, he may have a well-developed area (where the product has been sold for some time) whilst other sales people are selling in new areas of operation. This salesman might also be far more experienced than his colleagues.

This example shows some of the strengths and weaknesses of quantitative information. From a basic amount of data you can build up more information which, if calculated correctly, is as true as the original. For our salesman, the information that he is making two visits for each order is an accurate description of his performance. What we don't know from this information is WHY he is more successful!

Quantitative information can describe accurately what is happening. For example, it is possible to use some statistical techniques to find whether there is any relationship (known as correlation) between events.

Correlation shows that when one thing occurs, something else is likely to happen as well. What correlation can't do is to show why certain events do occur, or to prove what causes such events. You may well think that this isn't very important – if we know that some things tend to follow (or accompany) others, it doesn't matter why. Often this is true, but there are frequently cases in marketing when it is important to know what causes certain events to occur – to establish just what is cause and what is effect.

Look at the following marketing data relating to a chain of supermarkets in the United Kingdom.

● *Sales are 22 per cent higher on Friday than other days of the week.*
● *An extra £1m spent on advertising produced a 30 per cent increase in sales, increasing profits by £3.2m.*
● *In Scotland sales of red apples are higher than green apples, whereas* **in the South of England it's the reverse.**

You are the marketing manager of the chain of supermarkets. You are planning a new advertising campaign for the store's greengrocery. Why might you need to know the cause of these events? Stop reading and make a note of your ideas before continuing.

As we have already seen, advertising can easily be wasted money. Its purpose is to encourage particular patterns of behaviour, yet we need to understand that behaviour if we are to influence it. The first item of marketing data in the Activity above showed high sales on Fridays. If more people go shopping on Fridays, perhaps we could encourage that, to try to increase Friday sales even more. On the other hand, we could try to 'smooth out' the pattern of shopping across the week. We can't begin to do either unless we know something about *why* sales peak on one day.

In the case of the increased advertising expenditure, did the £1m extra have its effect simply because of the amount spent, or was it because the advertisements themselves were so well constructed and effective? Would £1m spent on different advertisements have the same effect?

When it comes to selling apples, should we feature both green and red apples nationwide to appeal to different tastes or should we make different distribution arrangements and advertisements for different parts of the country?

In all three cases the information available tells us *what*, it doesn't tell us *why*. The ability of quantitative market information to answer 'why' is limited; we draw inferences from information, but that's not the same as knowing why!

However it is possible, by commissioning market research, to gather qualitative information which can help to explain 'why'.

As we have already seen, quantitative information is numerical whereas qualitative information is descriptive. Qualitative information can't, for example, be multiplied or divided to calculate other valid information. What it can do is help you to understand why people behave in particular ways, what their feelings, attitudes, beliefs and motivations are. It can be very useful in helping sort out cause and effect. Of course, whether you can transfer conclusions based on information from one group of people to other groups is less certain than with quantitative information. We will look at this in more detail when we examine commissioned market research in Chapter 3.

The following market information is either qualitative or quantitative. In the box beside each item put a cross (✕) if you think it is qualitative, or a nought (0) if you think it is quantitative.

3–5 mins

1 *Sales this month are up by 55 on the same period last year.*
2 *The average value of a sale in a store is £1.32.*
3 *The sales force report that wholesalers have been impressed with the new advertising campaign.*
4 *13 per cent of housewives interviewed said they bought the product because it was 'tasty'.*
5 *A group of six housewives in an unstructured discussion about the product responded very favourably to the new flavour. They thought it more distinctive and less bitter than the old one, and suggested their children would prefer it.*

Compare your answers with the ones on page 128.

You will be looking at a whole range of information from now on, both quantitative and qualitative. Always keep in mind the difference between the two; as we will see in Chapter 3, the nature of the information being collected influences the whole approach to conducting, analysing and basing decisions on, commissioned market research.

In the next chapter we will be looking at the other elements of the market information system and seeing how each can help in preparing the ground for commissioning market research.

2 Preparing the Ground

After working through this chapter you will be able to identify the market information which can be obtained from manual and electronic record systems. You will also be able to explain why statistical and other mathematical models are important in forecasting market demand, and describe the main sources of market data available to desk researchers.

Where do you start?

In Chapter 1 we started to look at market research. We saw that it is concerned with all aspects of the marketing mix, and that it fits into a larger pattern of data collection and analysis, a Market Information System (MIS). Finally we saw that an MIS includes two essentially different types of information, quantitative and qualitative.

In this chapter we will concentrate on three areas of MIS:

● Marketing records
● Statistical and economic models
● Desk research

Each of these can help to prepare the ground for commissioned market research (the fourth part of MIS). Before setting out to collect information about the market directly, you will find out how to make the best use of information which is already available.

Only when you have made a full use of existing sources of data should you move on, as we will in Chapter 3, to look at how you can collect your own information by directly researching the market.

Marketing records

New organisations and organisations moving into new markets suffer from a major disadvantage: they don't know much about the buying behaviour of their potential customers. Filling in the gaps in their knowledge can be expensive since they may have to commission market research to discover patterns which organisations familiar with the market will know already. If those established organisations have effective systems for recording information about customers and their buying behaviour they will have gradually built up a valuable market database.

ACTIVITY

12

There is a range of information that all organisations must generate and collect in the course of their everyday operations. Some of this information can be very useful for marketing purposes.

Try your hand at identifying one or two examples. Make a note of your ideas, then read on.

2–3 mins

Organisations generate a range of information relevant to marketing, although the relevance may not always be obvious. Most accounting data (including stock control data) has a marketing application. At the very least this means records of income (or expenditure on activities, in parts of the public sector) which show patterns of demand on a daily, weekly, monthly, quarterly, or annual basis.

In a well-developed recording system you might have information about the value of business by customer or customer type, order size and frequency, geographical spread of business and so on.

The amount and type of information that can be collected in marketing records is determined by the nature of the marketing relationship between the organisation and its customers. With business customers and in some consumer transactions, far more information is available about the customer than is the case for most day-to-day consumer purchases. This means that in order to decide what information it is possible to collect which will be useful for marketing, we have to look carefully at each individual organisation.

ACTIVITY

13

5–10 mins

Choose an organisation which you know reasonably well, such as your bank, building society or insurance company. How much information does your chosen organisation normally collect about its customers or clients? Can you think of any evidence which shows this information is used to shape the products offered and marketing strategy used? Make some brief notes outlining your ideas.

We thought about the information a typical bank has about its personal account holders.

This would certainly include age, marital status and address. It would also be likely to include at least some indications about many other aspects of you and your lifestyle. For example, if your salary was paid into your account each month it would give an idea of your annual income. Mortgage payments would tell something about your major commitments. Facts such as a regular overdraft, or a large savings account, or share dividends paid regularly, are significant too.

Evidence of how the bank uses this information for marketing can come in a variety of guises. For example, what does the arrival of a letter offering you a gold credit card show?

Think about how the bank could use the information it holds on its customers when planning the marketing of the following products: personal pension plans, guaranteed overdraft schemes, mortgages, life insurance.

The Activity you have just completed confirms that an organisation can best understand its market when it knows who its customers are, so maintaining records about customers makes sense. With industrial business-to-business marketing these records are necessary for accounting purposes anyway – to maintain a sales ledger, give credit, issue invoices and so on. It makes sense to see such financial records as potential marketing records and not to establish separate record systems if a shared system is possible. Information technology contributes here by providing methods for storing, updating and cross-referencing data.

ACTIVITY

14

Make a list of all the items of basic information you might find it useful to keep about a customer if you were engaged in business-to-business marketing.

3 mins

The most obvious type of record you would need to keep on customers is a list of names, addresses, telephone numbers, contacts, etc. This could be in the form of a card index. The IT equivalent is the computer database which allows such information to be stored electronically. Figure 3 shows a printout of a simple customer record file written in a database program called dBase3. This is one of the most commonly used programs for handling this type of information, although many others are available which are essentially similar. Compare the items of information included in this customer record file with the list you drew up for Activity 14. Don't worry if they are not identical, but if the example includes items not in your list think about those you left off and consider what use they might be.

'Ah yes, Mr Smith . . . Your orders seem to have fallen . . . You're in 'Small customers' this month'.

Organising customers into different categories

A file created within a database can contain records of all an organisation's customers. This can then be sorted using any of the 'fields'

26

(items of information) contained in the file. For example names and addresses are two typical fields that can be sorted alphabetically,

```
Company          Abbeyvale Engineering
Address          Unit 2
                 Blackbush Trading Estate
                 Bristol
                 Avon
                 BS6 2GR

Contact1         John Grimshaw
Title1           Purchasing Manager
Contact2         Beryl Merryweather
Title2           Purchasing Asst.
Deladd1          Unit 2
Deladd2          Blackbush Trading Estate
Deltown          Bristol
Delcounty        Avon
Delpcode         BS6 2GR
Delcont          Warehouse Manager (Mr.Brett)
SIC              3253
Comments
Visit2wkly       N
Visit4wkly       Y
Visit8wkly       N
Lastvisit        1989/07/06
Lastordrc        1989/01/04
Lastordel        1989/12/06
Lastordval       1578.60
Cumval           4538.00
Totlastyr        30435.78
```

There are five elements to this customer file:

1   The company name, address and contacts.

2   Delivery details.

3   The Standard Industrial Classification (SIC) which identifies the customer's main business activity (in this case, manufacturing caravans) and an "open field" where comments can be made about the firm.

4   The Visit Cycle (two, four or eight weeks) indicated by Y (yes) or N (no), and most recent visit.

5   Order details, giving the date the last order was received, delivered, and its value, which automatically updates the cumulative value for the year to date, to compare with last year's total.

Figure 3 Dbase3+ record

geographically or by industry. By storing additional information such as frequency or value of orders it is possible to analyse the file to group customers into different categories. This could allow you to work out pricing or discount levels, to organise sales representative call frequency or to target direct mail or promotional offers.

Many companies now use an integrated accounting system with a customer database at its heart. This makes it far easier for organisations to assess the impact on their customers of all aspects of the marketing mix. Of course, the purpose of marketing is not just to generate demand but also to ensure that it is satisfied. Measuring how well an organisation can respond to demand is as important as measuring the level of demand generated. Failure to deliver a product, excessively long delivery periods, or high return rates, all reflect badly on the organisation and its marketing stance.

An organisation collects the following data about its sales transactions.

● *Date and number of enquiries*
● *Date, number, size and value of orders*
● *Date, number and size of deliveries*
● *Date, number and value of invoices*
● *Date, number, size and value of returns*

How could this information be used to measure its effectiveness in satisfying customers?

Compare your answers with the text which follows.

There are many ways in which data of this type can be used to measure organisational effectiveness. Figure 4 contains a list of commonly-used indicators derived from this information, which can help to assess how well a firm is performing in responding to the needs of the market. They are not the only indicators which can be used, nor would they all be useful in every case, but they can tell you a lot about how a firm is performing.

● Average time between enquiry and order/delivery/invoice.
● Average time between order and delivery/invoice.
● Proportion of enquiries converted into orders.
● Number of orders delivered in full or number of deliveries per order.
● Average size/value of orders/deliveries/invoices.
● Number of returns and reasons for returns.
● Rate of returns compared to orders, by frequency/size/value.

Figure 4 Indicators of marketing performance

For example, a firm which cares about its responsiveness to customer enquiries and orders could easily set targets for the times between enquiries and orders, or orders and delivery. It might also measure the effectiveness of its sales and promotion activities by the rate at which it converts enquiries into orders.

The ability of an organisation to meet all orders in full ensures satisfied customers; it also cuts costs in extra deliveries and paperwork, not to mention cancelled orders. It is obvious too, that the fixed costs of delivery, order processing and invoicing push up average costs if only small orders are being received. Keeping an eye on order size and value gives you the information to encourage sales staff to maximize both.

The last thing an organisation wants is to gain and then lose a sale because goods are returned, or services cancelled. The failure to satisfy customers adequately by inferior or faulty products makes the investment in marketing a wasted investment. Information on the number and proportion of returns allows you to keep track of the position in this vital area.

Most of the examples of the use of marketing records we have looked at have been in business-to-business markets, but organisations dealing with the general public can use exactly the same techniques. Three broad groups of organisations are most able to do this – those in the service sector, the consumer durables industry and those selling through mail order.

ACTIVITY

16

→←

1 min

Why should these three groups be able to use marketing records particularly effectively? What information about their customers or clients are such organisations likely to be able to collect?

As we noted when we looked at banking services in an earlier section, for industries in the service sector, such as insurance, education and training, or health care, it is common to obtain quite detailed (and often personal) information about customers, including age, sex, marital status, income, children, ethnicity and religion, as well as obvious details such as name and address. You can imagine how useful it will be for an organisation to know who its customers are at this level of detail. Using this information it can identify its existing market segments and engage in 'gap analysis' to identify the extent to which it is failing to penetrate the market fully, or to identify other markets it regards as having potential.

Less personal, but still valuable, details, are often available to organisations engaged in supplying other services or consumer durables, and those selling through mail order. The consumer's need for household delivery, maintenance, or the provision of credit, enables organisations to obtain details which can be used for customer analysis and to assist in subsequent direct marketing activity.

Techniques of analysis known as 'geodemographics' (see pages 78–79) contribute to this type of consumer profiling. The linking together of location with census details has made the identification and targeting of consumers a far more precise activity than ever before.

ACTIVITY

17

→←

3–5 mins

Think back to any recent major consumer purchase you have made. What information about you was collected (or could have been collected) as part of the transaction? Have you received any direct mail advertising recently; can you work out where the sender got your name and address from?

You have probably realised that the two parts of this Activity are not unconnected. Mailing lists prepared from names and addresses collected at the point of sale are commonly used to target direct mail at particular consumer groups. For example, if you bought any shares in government privatisation issues, you may well have found yourself receiving lots of unsolicited information about a wide range of financial services.

Many organisations make the mistake of ignoring the wealth of information available to them about their existing customer base. Before proceeding to ask questions about potential new customers it makes sense to identify who are the existing ones. Customer record systems are now a practical possibility for a large number of organisations. Care in establishing, maintaining and analysing such records is the first stage in the creation of an effective Market Information System.

Statistical and econometric models

You have already met a simple version of such a model in the first workbook in this course, although it wasn't described as such. The product life cycle is a statistical model, relating sales to time.

ACTIVITY

18

3 mins

Try sketching the shape of the product life cycle and label it with the names of four phases in a product's life.

Compare your sketch with the one on page 129.

The product life cycle reflects the pattern of demand for a product over its whole life (hence the name!). But within that cycle other patterns of demand may also be apparent which operate on shorter cycles. A cycle is the period during which the measurement of an observable phenomenon (in this case sales) fluctuates from, and returns to, a given level. In the case of a product life cycle the starting and finishing points are zero sales.

Many products also have a seasonal sales cycle, fluctuating according to the time of the year. Such seasonality can reflect, for example, climatic effects (overcoats in winter, ice cream in summer) or it can be caused by an event which is itself seasonal. For example, there isn't much demand for Easter eggs in October, or Christmas cards in March. Marketing activity can often be aimed at diminishing 'natural' seasonal patterns, to try to even out demand and make supply easier (by not bunching production or having to hold large stocks). Cadburys have had a great success in stretching the sales of their Creme Eggs back to the end of December! It is also possible to stimulate 'artificial' seasonal fluctuations, by encouraging peaks in demand to balance out troughs in the demand for other products supplied by the organisation.

ACTIVITY

19

5–10 mins

Consider electricity sales. Are there likely to be seasonal fluctuations in demand? If so, do local electricity boards attempt to stimulate or depress demand through marketing activity? Sketch out on the diagram below an outline of how you think sales would fluctuate throughout the year.

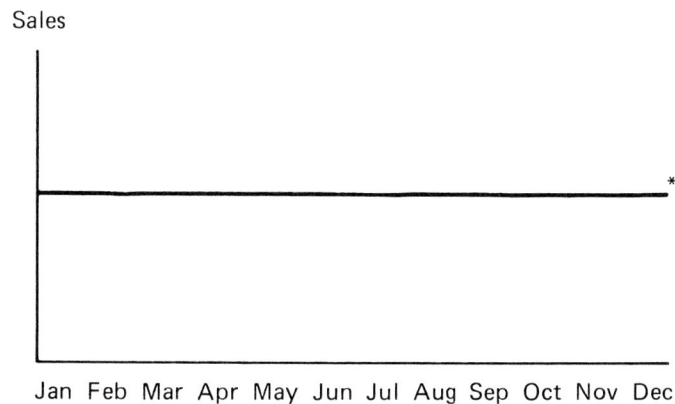

Sales

Jan Feb Mar Apr May Jun Jul Aug Sep Oct Nov Dec

*What a sales curve would look like if sales were constant through the year.

Figure 5

Compare your answer with the one on page 129.

The shape of a product life cycle is a long term pattern usually described as a trend, to distinguish it from shorter cycles, such as those caused by seasonal fluctuations. The ability to forecast both long and short term patterns of demand is essential for any organisation, since the sales forecast figures on a monthly or quarterly basis will provide an organisation with the source for its longer term forecasts of income, production and profits.

The simplest forecasts can be based on the supplier's expert knowledge and experience of the market. For some industrial goods, particularly very high priced and low volume items, this can be all that is needed.

For the majority of products, however, a more sophisticated analysis of the market is usually required. Here statistical techniques are of value. This book is not concerned with teaching statistics and you won't be shown how to calculate forecasts, but we will look at an example to see how such techniques can be used.

Figure 6 shows an example of a simple forecasting technique using a 'moving average'. The moving average helps to identify the trend of sales and by projecting forward or extrapolating this moving average the next year's sales can be assessed. The moving average projected into the future is shown by the broken line on the graph.

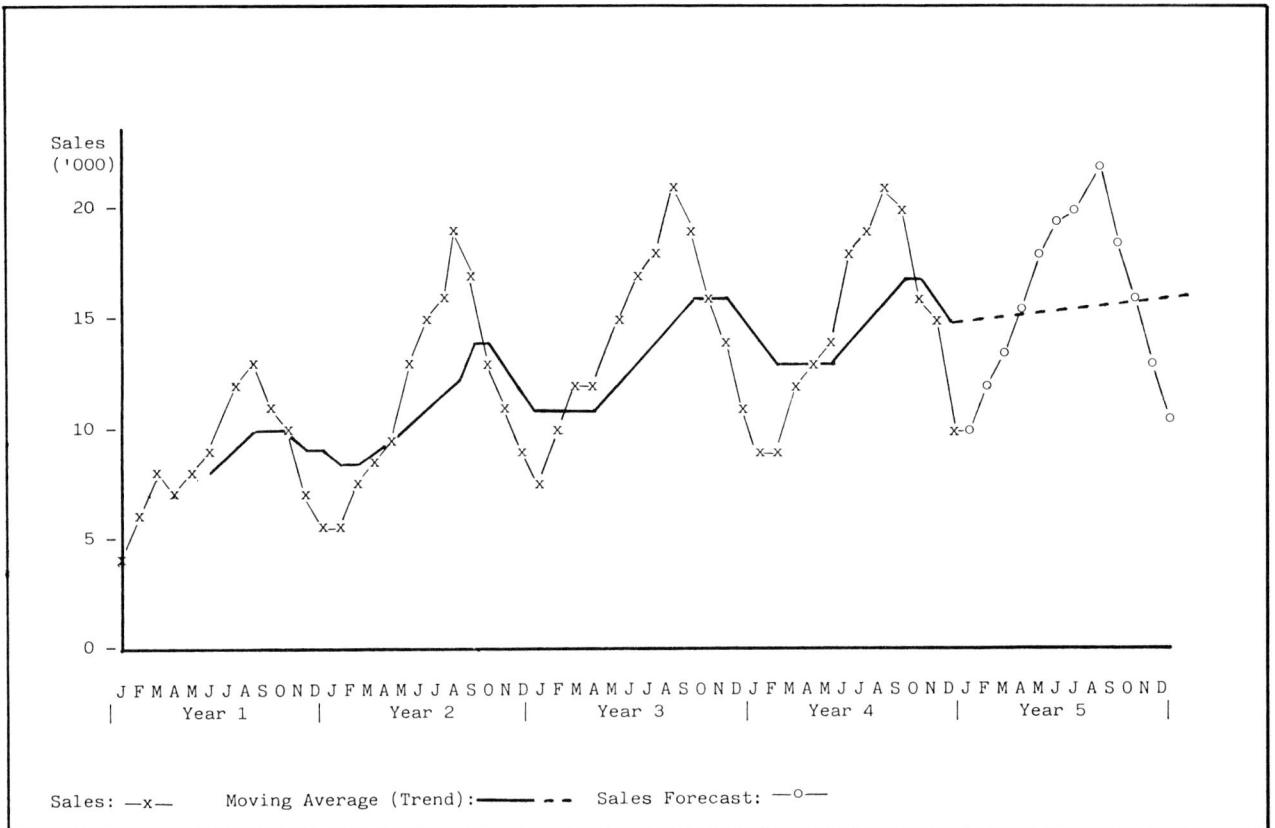

Figure 6 Sales forecasting using a moving average

In the example shown in Figure 6 the product is in the early part of its life cycle and sales are still growing. In forecasting future sales, judgement has to be made about how large the total market is and what share this product can expect to achieve. This will determine when sales will level out as the product reaches maturity.

The graph also shows a seasonal fluctuation in sales. In the final sales forecast the trend line has to be adjusted in order to take account of this.

ACTIVITY

20

3 mins

Which of the following do you think might be represented by the sales figures in Figure 6?

- *Ladies' boots*
- *Dog food*
- *Garden implements*
- *Coal*
- *Motor oil*
- *Hand cream*

Compare your answer with the one on page 129.

The actual demand for a product is the result of a variety of factors. Those we have already looked at – position on the life cycle and any seasonal characteristics – are of major importance. But so too may be the price and the price of other comparable products, the effects of marketing activity, fashion trends, interest rates, weather and even changes in population.

At its most sophisticated, forecasting can attempt to include all these determinants of demand in a complex computer program. Such programs, called 'econometric models', simulate customer behaviour mathematically and predict how sales will respond under various conditions. The cost of creating and maintaining such systems (the programs and the data required for them to be useful) is very high however, and is only justified in large organisations which already have large information systems. With less complex systems you will have to rely on informed judgements – using the knowledge and experience of staff to make assessments of the impact on sales of a price rise, for example.

ACTIVITY

21

Look again at Figure 6. It assumes that sales will go on rising in year five. What activity by a competitor might stop this?

2–3 mins   *Compare your answer with the one on page 129.*

You will by now have begun to appreciate that no matter how sophisticated the system of forecasting in use, it is very often the marketing or sales staff themselves who are best able to make the final decisions about the likely level of demand.

It is important to realise too that these modelling techniques are only as good as the information on which they are based. If you feed inaccurate information into a model, you will get inaccurate information out. (The computer industry has a useful expression for this – 'garbage in, garbage out'!)

Once sales forecasts have been produced the fact that they are quantitative makes them appear very certain. This means they look as if they must be right because they are so exact. This is often referred to as false, or 'spurious' objectivity. It makes sense to use other data, perhaps of a qualitative type, to check forecasts, and then to round them up or down to what appears realistic.

After all, sales forecasts are meant to be just that, forecasts of what will happen, not wishful dreams!

Desk research

In this section we will look at ways in which an organisation can research its market using easily accessible existing sources of information. You will find out about the types and sources of data available, and the uses to which desk research can be put. In particular you will find out the value of this type of research, either on its own or used as a guide to commissioning further research into the market.

As the name desk research suggests, collecting this information doesn't involve 'fieldwork' – going out to collect data from people directly – but rather that it can be carried out at your desk. (In practice it may well mean a library desk.)

Let's look first at sources of data. The people (or organisations) from whom information was originally collected are known as the *primary* sources. Desk research is based on 'second-hand' data from reference books, published survey data etc. It is therefore said to come from *secondary* sources. You may be surprised to learn how much information is available from these secondary sources, much of it free! What is more, this secondary data has already been collected and analysed so that it's possible to use it to arrive quickly at useful conclusions about the market.

ACTIVITY

22

Before reading on, jot down any advantages and disadvantages you think might arise from using desk research instead of commissioning original research from the primary sources.

3–5 mins

As advantages of desk research, you might have mentioned the lower cost, the possibility of avoiding the duplication of work already done, and the opportunity offered to researchers to clarify their ideas about the market before embarking on more detailed research.

As disadvantages, you probably spotted the danger of spending time searching fruitlessly for information which turns out not to exist, or finding information which is ambiguous or difficult to interpret. It is also possible to find data which is relevant and clear, but which is not based on good primary evidence, and therefore misleading. In the following paragraphs we will look at these advantages and disadvantages in more detail.

First of all the advantages. Desk research costs less than it would cost to conduct the original research using primary sources, but is it actually free? And if research has already been done are there no circumstances in which it should be duplicated?

In both cases the answers are 'no'.

ACTIVITY

23

Can you identify any reasons why desk research may not be 'free', or any occasions when a researcher might want to duplicate research someone else has carried out? Write a sentence or two to explain your ideas and then compare them with our comments below.

3 mins

Although desk research is much cheaper than commissioning original research, you shouldn't ignore the cost of the time involved in conducting it. This can easily run into days or even weeks. This time commitment is often called the 'opportunity cost' of the research. By undertaking it, the opportunity to do other work is lost. It isn't true either that all information is free to use; some specialist sources (such as the computer databases we will be looking at on page 40) can charge quite large fees for access.

Avoiding the duplication of previous research is clearly sensible; why repeat perfectly good research when you can learn from the work of others? There are some circumstances however when repetition may be necessary. This might be to confirm results, or to check that results are still the same after a period of time or that they apply to a different group of people.

We've looked at two of the advantages, but what about the third? Desk research can also clarify issues, helping researchers identify the nature of the problems to be resolved. This process is described as establishing a *hypothesis* to be tested. A hypothesis is a sort of 'informed guess'. It may be, for example, that 'customers for a particular product are more likely to be above a certain age' or 'firms with more than 100 employees are likely to be interested in a new service'. In other words, desk research can lead us to tentative conclusions about the market which we want to use commissioned research to back up.

For example, a company may decide to establish a nationwide service to delivery disposable nappies to homes. It believes that by buying in bulk and operating local distribution centres it can undercut retailers and offer the convenience of home delivery of a very bulky commodity. Initial desk research could identify existing and projected birth rates, published research into the advantages of disposable compared with reusable nappies, and the typical number of nappy changes per baby. From this information an initial hypothesis about the likely market size could be made. Further commissioned reearch could then explore the likely demand within the total market for the proposed service.

ACTIVITY

24

✳

5–10 mins

As we have said, a hypothesis is an intelligent guess about how certain things relate to one another. It is intelligent because it is based on existing information, however sketchy that information might be.

Imagine that you are involved in the marketing of a familiar product – an environmentally friendly washing powder, or the latest model of a sporty hatchback, or any other item that takes your fancy.

Make an intelligent guess about who uses the product (age, sex, social class, marital status etc could all be relevant factors). Try writing down your guess in the form of an hypothesis along the lines:

> *'potential purchasers of the Thunderflier XRJS convertible are likely to be males under 30 with an above average income.'*

Try discussing your hypothesis with friends or colleagues who might also be interested in the product, to see if they agree with you.

While not all research can or should fit this pattern it is often the most sensible approach to adopt. In some cases hypotheses will arise from other sources (e.g. from the pattern of sales, or from customer records), but the ideas involved can still be explored further by desk research before going directly into commissioned research.

We have already summarised some of the disadvantages of desk research. Perhaps the worst experience is to spend hours, days or even weeks looking for non-existent information! Or finding information which is ambivalent, ambiguous or unclear. Clearly this sort of outcome is wasteful. Fortunately most experienced researchers know when to stop; common sense will often tell you when the exercise is not worth pursuing.

. . . most experienced researchers know when to stop . . .

Problems can also arise when data is contradictory, or suggests the market would behave in a way you think is highly unlikely. There is a strong temptation to disregard information which you don't expect to hear!

There is a strong temptation to disregard information which you don't expect to hear

Equally, you shouldn't blindly accept research results without question; that would be foolish. You must approach all research with an open mind and take note of all information; you then have to make your own judgements.

A famous example of this is the Sony Walkman. Some years ago the Japanese electronics company Sony researched the market potential for a small stereo tape player with no recording facility. All the evidence suggested that consumers would not buy a machine which would only play back; despite that Sony went ahead and the Walkman was born, one of the most successful innovations ever in consumer electronics.

ACTIVITY

25

5 mins

There is an important 'lesson' to be learned from the example of the Sony Walkman and the use of research in marketing. Can you spot what it is?

Compare your answer with the one on page 130.

Now that we have looked at some of the features of desk research, we can begin to consider how to go about it. The first stage is to identify what it is you want to know. Statements like 'all about the market' or 'what I can find out about my competitors' are far too vague. You must be prepared to take such generalisations and refine them into specific areas for investigation and precise questions to be answered.

ACTIVITY

26

5 mins

Choose a consumer product you know fairly well – perhaps one that you have used in earlier activities.

You want to know 'all about the market' for the product. Try writing down three or four questions, the answers to which will start you on the road to knowing 'all about the market'.

The questions you chose to replace 'all about the market' might have included:

- Which firms are currently in the market?
- What is the total size of the market?
- How much do consumers spend annually on this type of product (or product group)?
- How is the population in a particular age, or geographical area, or social class group, likely to change over the next five years?

Questions like these and any others you thought of are more likely to lead to clear answers and will help direct you to appropriate sources of information. A series of such questions may well add up to 'all about the market' but they are far more likely to produce coherent and usable information.

Activity 26, and the discussion which followed, illustrate the many specific questions it may be necessary to ask to give you all the information you would like. Such an exercise also helps by allowing you to distinguish what it is you *must* know from what you would *like to* know. By identifying priorities in this way, the time and effort devoted to the research can then be allocated so that more time is spent finding out about the more important issues.

Desk research – sources of information

Having decided what information we want, we now have to identify likely sources. Most larger public libraries contain a reference section full of publications which will almost certainly be of use. Which organisation do you think is likely to be the largest publisher of data, particularly statistical data, about the United Kingdom?

There are no prizes for spotting that this massive source of data is the government. This is also true in most other countries, where you should look first to official sources for general data about the marketplace.

Information published by the United Kingdom government can be loosely divided into two types, *regular* series of monthly, quarterly or annual publications, and *occasional* ones which are produced on specific topics, such as circulars, official reports and policy statements. Some of these publications consist almost entirely of tables of statistics, others contain commentaries, analyses and articles alongside statistical data, and some have little or no statistical content.

To find out about the full range of regularly published data, try to visit a larger public or college library. There you should be able to locate sources such as *Annual Abstract of Statistics, Social Trends, Family Expenditure Survey (FES), and General Household Survey (GHS)*.

If you have any difficulty finding them, the library staff will be happy to help. Skim briefly through each in turn to get a feel for the type of information included.

You should also be able to look through the *Guide to Official Statistics* (Central Statistical Office: HMSO 1986), which will give you an idea of the range of data available. The Guide also tells you something about the Government Statistical Service and the Central Statistical Office, and about further sources of advice and information within various ministries and departments.

9.7 Journey purpose [1]: by main mode [2] of transport, 1985–86

Great Britain

Percentages and thousands

| | Public transport | | | Private transport | | | | | Number of journeys in sample (= 100%) (thousands) | As a percentage of all journeys |
	Rail	Bus	Other	Car, van, lorry	Motor cycle	Bicycle	Walk [3]	Other		
Purpose of journey *(percentages)*										
To and from work	5	11	1	67	3	6	6	1	84.2	23
In course of work	3	1	1	87	1	2	2	2	11.9	3
Education	3	24	1	33	—	6	20	12	21.2	6
Escort for work	—	—	—	98	—	—	1	1	8.0	2
Escort for education	—	3	1	83	—	1	12	—	8.3	2
Shopping	1	18	1	66	1	3	11	—	71.9	19
Personal business	1	10	2	75	1	2	9	1	46.4	13
Social and entertainment	1	9	2	76	1	3	7	1	97.0	26
Holidays, day trips and other	2	2	2	54	1	3	34	2	19.9	5
All purposes	2	11	1	69	1	3	10	2	368.8	100

1 See Appendix, Part 9: Journey purpose.
2 The mode used for the greater part of the journey.

3 Excludes walks under 1 mile.

Source: National Travel Survey, 1985-86, Department of Transport

Social Trends 18, © Crown copyright 1988

(reproduced with the permission of the Controller of HMSO)

Figure 7

ACTIVITY 27

15 mins

Figure 7 is taken from the 1988 edition of Social Trends. *It shows the purposes people had when taking various forms of transport, and is an extract from the National Transport Survey, 1985–6, carried out by the Department of Transport.*

You are thinking of setting up a new bus company and you want to know what the pattern of demand is likely to be. What information can you extract from the table to show you:

a) *how many bus journeys in total were included in the table?*
b) *what were the two most popular reasons for travelling by bus, and how many bus journeys each did these account for?*

(Notice that the percentages add up horizontally and are based on the number of journeys in the ninth column, which is 'thousands of journeys'. The exception is the last column which adds up vertically and shows the purpose of journeys as a percentage of all journeys.)

Compare your conclusions with those on page 130.

As you have found out, there is a wealth of useful information in this table. From it, you could have learned something about your likely market, about making your bus timetables attractive to customers, and what to emphasise in your advertising. All this from one easily available table!

As well as official sources of data, there are lots of non-governmental sources you can use. You could start with the *Guide to Unofficial UK Statistics* (Mort & Siddall: Gower 1985); you will also find that a large range of directories exist, some of which can help to direct you to detailed sources. For the beginner in desk research, libraries and librarians can be of immense help in suggesting sources.

ACTIVITY

28

For this Activity, you need a copy of a local trade directory (for example Yellow Pages *or* Thompson's*). You are setting up in business to supply material to plumbers and heating contractors; what types of information can you find out about your competitors and your likely customers from this source?*

10–15 mins

Compare your findings with ours on page 130.

As you can see, a large amount of information can be obtained from a very mundane source; much more detailed and valuable information is likely to be available in specialist publications.

Print is not the only way of storing information; other sources involve the use of the most up-to-date technology for storage and retrieval of data. You may already know the broadcast teletext services available on some television sets (*Ceefax* on BBC, *Oracle* on ITV) which are accessible at no charge. You may have heard of the Prestel service available from British Telecom and electronic mail such as Telecom Gold, which use telephone lines linked to computers (through gadgets called modems). Prestel and Telecom Gold are just two of the range of services now available using electronic data storage and retrieval. They rely on the fact that it is possible to hold vast quantities of information (the database) very easily in computers and to get at that information quickly using telecommunications links.

The database can be stored anywhere (there are specialist companies like Prestel in London, or Dialog in California who have computers which 'host' databases produced by other organisations). To access these databases, your microcomputer is linked to the 'database' computer by telephone line and is then a part of it! Your micro has become a terminal.

Searching for information in a database is fairly straightforward; if you know where something is in a database you ask for it to be retrieved via your computer terminal. The information can be displayed on the screen, or printed out. If you don't know where the relevant information is (or even if it exists) you can ask for a 'keyword' search, and the computer will search for items which contain your key word(s).

Through these services you can gain access to some very specialist databases; they can be expensive to use but this cost needs to be set against the costs of collecting data from primary sources and analysing it yourself. To find out more about such facilities look at *Brit-line* (published by EDI Ltd in partnership with ICL) in most main libraries. This is a directory containing details of nearly all such databases available in the United Kingdom.

Figure 8 contains an example of a printout from one such electronic database, Target Group Index (TGI), produced by the British Market Research Bureau (BMRB). TGI is an example of an omnibus survey. We will discuss omnibus surveys in more detail later. It is stored on BMRB's own computer, and on some other 'host' computers, and organisations which subscribe to the service can have access to the database whenever they wish. There is an annual subscription charge and additional charges for using the database.

```
10/10/89                          BMRB'S CHOICES SYSTEM
                              BRITISH MARKET RESEARCH BUREAU

                                 1989 TGI SPECIAL ANALYSIS


SOURCE: TGI 89  WGT: POPB
TABLE BASE: ALL ADULTS

                                                        DRAUGHT    SCOTCH
                                      GIN -    VODKA -  LAGER -    WHISKY -
                                      FREQ:    FREQ:    FREQ:      FREQ:
                                      HEAVY    HEAVY    HEAVY      HEAVY
ROW                 CELL     TOTAL    USERS    USERS    USERS      USERS
-----------------   -------  -------  -------  -------  -------    -------

TOTAL               #RESP    24058    1025     978      916        1757
                    (000)    45122    2050     1711     1762       3320
                    VERT%    100.00   100.00   100.00   100.00     100.00
                    HORZ%    100.00   4.54     3.79     3.90       7.36
                    INDEX    100      100      100      100        100

SPORTS YOU PLAY     #RESP    1163     * 33     83       185        72
THESE DAYS: FOOTBALL (000)   2397     67       161      393        144
(ASSOCIATION)       VERT%    5.31     3.27     9.41     22.30      4.34
                    HORZ%    100.00   2.80     6.72     16.40      6.01
                    INDEX    100      62       177      419        82

SPORTS YOU PLAY     #RESP    1593     110      99       161        197
THESE DAYS: GOLF    (000)    3199     255      207      310        419
                    VERT%    7.09     12.44    12.10    17.59      12.62
                    HORZ%    100.00   7.97     6.47     9.69       13.10
                    INDEX    100      176      171      248        178

SPORTS YOU PLAY     #RESP    1891     67       137      233        142
THESE DAYS: DARTS   (000)    3578     127      216      432        271
                    VERT%    7.93     6.20     12.62    24.52      8.16
                    HORZ%    100.00   3.55     6.04     12.07      7.57
                    INDEX    100      78       159      309        103

SPORTS YOU PLAY     #RESP    1364     79       79       85         80
THESE DAYS: TENNIS  (000)    2751     145      146      182        181
                    VERT%    6.10     7.07     8.53     10.33      5.45
                    HORZ%    100.00   5.27     5.31     6.62       6.58
                    INDEX    100      116      140      169        89

SPORTS YOU PLAY     #RESP    1293     88       66       108        105
THESE DAYS: SQUASH  (000)    2601     162      134      217        211
                    VERT%    5.76     7.90     7.83     12.32      6.36
                    HORZ%    100.00   6.23     5.15     8.34       8.11
                    INDEX    100      137      136      213        110


* Projection relatively unstable because of sample base - use with caution

Copyright 1989 Target Group Index
```

Figure 8

You are the marketing manager for a whisky distiller and have been approached by promoters of amateur football, golf, darts, tennis and squash tournaments for sponsorship. Using the data in Figure 8, which would you agree to and why?

Compare your answers with the ones on page 131.

Other, non-electronic sources of specialist information include:

● Trade and professional associations and institutes;
● Specialist journals and magazines;
● Specialist libraries and information services.

Organisations often belong to trade associations of one sort or another, many of which collect and publish information of interest to their members. Equally there are specialist institutes and associations to which individuals can belong and which offer similar services. To use them you don't always have to be a member, although some information may only be available to members, or may be charged at higher prices to non-members.

There are a host of specialist journals and magazines published, aimed at most trades, professions etc, and these contain lots of valuable information about the market.

There are a host of specialist journals and magazines . . .

ACTIVITY

30

*

10–15 mins

Look for a specialist journal in your local library or newsagent; it could be a trade magazine like The Grocer or a special interest magazine like those for computer users. Make a list of any types of information in there which might be of interest to a firm in that market. This could be about new products from rival suppliers, new outlets opening, or market trends for example.

Associations, institutes and the publishers of journals and magazines often have libraries or information services you can use. There are also organisations founded purely to give out information, like the Independent Schools Information Service or the British Trout Information Bureau. However, you need to be careful if you use these sources. The function of these organisations is often to promote their sponsors, which can make them selective in the information they provide.

The desk researcher can use the whole range of sources described above to investigate the market; many will be of little use, some may simply suggest other sources. But undoubtedly it is possible to amass substantial information about the market, at minimum cost.

Conclusion

In Chapter 2 we have explored three of the four main sources of market information:

- marketing records;
- statistical and econometric models;
- desk research.

By now you will be able to see how each relates to the others. Our records of customer purchases can be related to market size through desk research. Or an aspect of the market identified by desk research can be included in the econometric model developed by an organisation. The information required by statisticians will come from marketing records and predictions about the growth of the total market can be measured against published data.

ACTIVITY

31

30–40 mins

In this Activity, we are going to bring together the three types of market information discussed in this chapter. Examples of each type are given in Figures 9–12 on the next page. Your task is to use the data provided to prepare a short report (no more than 200 words) on the market and the firm's response to it. See how much you can conclude about the organisation and the opportunities open to it. Compare your report with the one we have prepared on page 131 when you have finished.

We haven't said anything about what the product is. You might find it helpful to think of a 'real' product of your own choice when preparing the report.

Figure 9 Product sales (years 1–3) and sales forecasts (years 4–5)   *(£m)*

Month	J	F	M	A	M	J	J	A	S	O	N	D	
Year													
1	0.6	0.9	1.2	1.5	1.6	1.6	1.7	1.8	1.7	1.5	1.7	1.4	17.2
2	1.5	1.6	1.6	1.7	1.7	1.8	1.8	1.7	1.9	1.7	1.8	1.5	20.3
3	1.6	1.6	1.7	1.6	1.7	1.7	1.8	1.9	1.8	1.8	1.7	1.5	20.4
4	1.5	1.6	1.6	1.7	1.7	1.7	1.8	1.8	1.9	1.8	1.7	1.5	20.3
5	1.6	1.6	1.6	1.7	1.7	1.7	1.8	1.9	1.9	1.8	1.7	1.5	20.5

Figure 10 Industry sales (years 1–3) and forecasts (years 4–5)

Year	Forecast sales (£m)
1	68.7
2	74.3
3	80.2
4	87.1
5	91.2

Figure 11 Summary from Sales Manager's annual report

'The retail trade were very receptive to the new product when it was launched but they have begun to be resistant. Our prices are higher than many of our competitors and our advertising and promotion activity does not seem to have been as effective at stimulating demand from customers. It is also worth noting that several of our competitors now offer a 48hr delivery service!'

Figure 12 Delivery data (analysis January to May, year 3)

Order to delivery time (days)	Proportion of total orders (%)
1	7
2	19
3	30
4	21
5	11
6–8	5
9–14	2
Cancelled	5
	100

FIRST PROGRESS TEST

Try to answer the questions below without referring to the text. When you have finished, compare your answers with the ones on page 141, then if you are happy with your score, move on to Chapter 3.

1 Complete the following sentence:

Market research is the process by which an organisation investigates its

.... (or ....)

to assess reaction to ....,

.... and ....

2 What are the four parts of MIS?

a)
b)
c)
d)

3 Which of the following statements provide quantitative information?

a) Six times a week
b) Not as often as I'd like
c) Every Friday, without fail
d) Whenever I can
e) Two or three times a year

4 Complete the following sentence:

An organisation's .... are based on existing information about the customer.

5 The product life cycle is an example of:

seasonal sales fluctuations
a statistical model
a marketing technique
a sales forecast
secondary data

3 Commissioned Market Research

After working through this chapter you will be able to describe the main steps involved in designing and using a market research project and explain the importance of questionnaire design and sampling strategy. You will also be able to recognise the main methods of customer classification, and describe the contribution which omnibus surveys can make to a market research strategy.

Introduction

Most of the modern features of marketing such as sales forces, advertising and advertising agencies, and standardised products for a mass market, can be traced to the eighteenth and nineteenth centuries when the onset of industrialisation replaced those forms of business relying on individual craftsmen. The introduction of market research was also a consequence of this same process, although it didn't make an appearance until the early part of the twentieth century.

Industrialisation involves large-scale production, requiring large markets to match. It relies on efficient distribution systems, and the support of promotion and pricing strategies – in other words, the marketing mix!

ACTIVITY

32

Can you think of one important reason why market research also developed as a consequence of the industrialisation process? Make a note of your answer, then read on.

3 mins

Industrialisation led to a lengthening of the communication channels between producer and consumer. Attempts to improve the effectiveness of these channels involved the development of both advertising and of networks of wholesale and retail outlets. These enabled producers to bring products to the attention of the public and make them available locally.

But these improvements in the communication process did not work equally in both directions. They helped the producer get the message about a product to the consumer, but they did little to improve the feedback the producer got from the consumer.

Although some signals did come back from the market, from customers' willingness to buy or not to buy, these were rather crude, and only occurred after production decisions had been made. What's more, in those industries where consumers had little choice (for example, in some public sector activities), those signals were often totally inadequate.

Market research evolved to fill the communications gap by enabling suppliers to obtain replies from the market to the questions they needed to ask. We have seen the part played by desk research in filling this communications gap; commissioned market research can play an even larger role by ensuring clearer answers are given to more specific questions.

We shall look at the process of commissioned market research in this chapter, under six main headings:

- market research design;
- questionnaire design;
- classifying consumers;
- sampling the market;
- omnibus surveys;
- research analysis and application.

In this way you will see how a research project is built up and conducted, and the ways in which the data collected can be used to determine marketing strategies.

●●●

CASE STUDY: *The Independent*

From its original inception until its eventual launch, market research was used to help the founders of *The Independent* in their new product development.

Because newspapers rely on two customers – their readers and the advertising agencies which buy space for their clients – it was important that a clearly defined market existed, and one which was appealing to the advertisers.

The advertising agency Saatchi and Saatchi advised *The Independent*'s Editor and Chief Executive Andreas Whittam Smith from the project's inception and commissioned research from Research Surveys of Great Britain Ltd to investigate attitudes to existing newspapers amongst 25–44 year-olds.

Subsequent research revealed that the name alone was important in determining expectations about the paper. Names like *The Examiner* and *The Chronicle* suggested an older people's newspaper, *The Arena* or *24 Hours*, one with a youthful, modern image. The choice of *The Independent* (young, balanced politically, open-minded) reflected the editorial policy initially established. As Whittam Smith had said, the paper would be 'market researched, but editorial-led'.

Various possible designs – layout, typefaces, etc. were also subjected to research, and during the vital month before launch, dummies (test versions) of the paper were supplied to a consumer panel. 320 respondents maintained diaries, were telephone surveyed and, finally, personally interviewed to assess their reactions to both layout and content. This helped to clarify the balance needed between different areas of coverage, and the way such topic areas are presented. It also confirmed a generally positive reaction to the new paper.

After its launch, continuous research was used to measure the reader's (and non reader's) reactions. One week after the first issue appeared, 2000 respondents were telephone surveyed, a quota sample of 1200 AB and 800 CI readers (see page 85). This explored not only what they liked and disliked about the paper, but also which paper they had switched from. It is indicative of the care and attention to detail with which *The Independent* was developed, that in a market with exceedingly high brand loyalty, the paper was able to establish its market position by convincing a quarter of a million people to switch papers and to remain loyal to the new product.

●●●

Market research design

Commissioning and designing a market research project can be a complex process.

In this section we will look at the process to explain *why* things are done the way they are. We will not be telling you *how* to do it. The idea is to give you enough insight into the activities involved to be able to commission a research project effectively.

ACTIVITY

33

2–3 mins

Which of these questions are likely to be useful as a starting point for commissioning market research? Can you explain why?

a) *In what age range is the typical consumer for our product?*
b) *What factors make our products attractive?*
c) *What will be the most effective colour for the product pack?*
d) *How much benefit will we get from advertising the product?*

Compare your answers with ours on page 131.

As we saw in the last chapter, research, however it is conducted, will only be effective if you identify specific questions to be dealt with – 'How many people do this?' or 'What do people think about that?' Commissioning any form of consumer or business survey requires exactly the same approach. The first step in designing a market research project is to identify the questions you want answered. We saw this earlier, in the ABTA case study (page 15) where ABTA wanted to know what customers felt about the services offered by its members to package holidaymakers.

This doesn't mean that we have to establish at this stage the questions to be included in the survey. As we will see later, the design of such questions is a different and specialised task. What it does mean is identifying the precise issues to be addressed by the research: what information is actually needed? You also need to decide how to go about having your questions answered. If you have exhausted the possibilities of desk research, and other aspects of your own market information systems, you will need to look to a market research agency.

ACTIVITY

34

➤⟵

5–10 mins

Hadley Health Centre is a General Practice serving the medical needs of most of the population of the small town of Hadley. It is staffed by doctors, community midwives and health visitors, and has its own dispensary.

The members of the practice are concerned as to how well they are **meeting the needs of their clients (their patients) in the range and nature of** *the services they provide.*

They are thinking of approaching a market researcher to undertake some research into this. Write down four questions you think they want the researcher to find answers to.

Compare your questions with the ones suggested on page 131.

Most agencies employ professional researchers who are members of the Market Research Society (or the Industrial Market Research Association for specialist business researchers). These organisations can supply details of agencies employing their members. This is important, because it gives you a guarantee of the quality of their work, and the validity of the process used. In Figure 13 you will see an extract from the MRS Code of Conduct, which includes a statement of its basic principles. Agencies vary in size and location; some also conduct the opinion polls published in newspapers, magazines and on television, which you will undoubtedly have seen.

Figure 13 Market Research Society Code of Conduct

'Research is founded upon the willing co-operation of the public and of business organisations. It depends upon public and business confidence that it is conducted honestly, objectively, without unwelcome intrusion and without harm to informants. Its purpose is to collect and analyse information, and not directly to create sales nor to influence the opinions of anyone participating in it. It is in this spirit that the Code of Conduct has been devised.

'The general public and other interested parties shall be entitled to complete assurance that every research project is carried out strictly in accordance with this Code, and that their rights of privacy are respected.

'In particular, they must be assured that no information which could be used to identify them will be made available without their agreement to anyone outside the agency responsible for conducting the research. They must also be assured that the information they supply will not be used for any purposes other than research and that they will in no way be adversely affected or embarrassed as a direct result of their participation in a research project.

'Finally, the research findings themselves must always be reported accurately and never mislead anyone, in any way.'

ACTIVITY

35

✽

Over the next few days look out for an example of an opinion poll in your daily newspaper, or a magazine or on television. Look to see the name of the firm responsible for conducting it. Were any details given of sample size, sampling method or questions used?

Selecting an appropriate agency depends on several factors, which you have to consider carefully. Many of these organisations are based in London, although there are agencies, often smaller firms, all over the United Kingdom. Depending where you are, you may have to judge between convenience and size. Some agencies specialise, others cover most apsects of the work. You will find that the cost of agencies varies, so it makes sense to talk to more than one before coming to a decision.

Some MR agencies are connected to advertising agencies and if your advertising agency offers such a service you may be attracted by the convenience of such a link.

Alternatively, you may wish to investigate other sources to find the most suitable provider of services to meet your needs.

Usually you will work with a representative of the agency, called a research executive, who manages the design and conduct of the research and liaises with you as a client. The relationship is much the same as you would experience with an account executive in an advertising agency.

ACTIVITY

36

10 mins

Draw up a list of five or six key factors you would need to consider when deciding on the most appropriate MR agency. Compare this with the list on page 132.

Having decided on your agency, and having briefed them on your requirements – the questions you want answered – you may find they do not necessarily recommend some form of survey straight away. Possibly they will urge further analysis of your existing data on the market (sales figures, customer records, etc.) They may also propose some more sophisticated desk research than you have so far conducted.

They may even suggest you are asking the wrong questions! One advantage an agency has is its opportunity to talk to a variety of organisations, and to build up its own knowledge of the market. This independent advice can be of great value in identifying the key issues to be addressed during the research.

ACTIVITY

37

15 mins

Somerset Sou'westers plc has been selling a range of waterproof clothing to professional seafarers for many years. They have decided to expand into the amateur sailors' market and into the market for land-based leisure enthusiasts (hikers, etc.) They have decided to commission research into the market's attitude to their products and the likely market size this suggests.

You are a research executive approached to conduct the MR envisaged. What advice would you give, before conducting a survey? Compare your answer with the one on page 132.

Once it has been decided that some form of commissioned market research is appropriate for a client's needs, an agency is able to draw on a wide range of research designs to obtain information from the market. We shall look briefly at the eight most commonly employed techniques; they are summarised in Figure 15 on page 58. A particular research design can employ any one of these techniques or variations on them, or they can be combined to meet particular needs.

Personal interviews

The conventional image of MR is of an interviewer with a clipboard asking questions of a respondent in the street or at home. Such interviews, using an interview schedule, or list of questions, are conducted face-to-face and

	CODE	ROUTE

IF ANY ANSWERS TO Q.23b, ASK: (OTHERS GO TO Q.27)

Q.24 In your opinion, whose fault was it that these things went wrong?
CODE ALL THAT APPLY.

	CODE	ROUTE
TOUR COMPANY	1	
HOTELIERS, PEOPLE RUNNING ACCOMODATION	2	
AIRLINES	3	
AIR TRAFFIC CONTROLLERS, AIRPORTS	4	
DK	5	
NOBODY'S FAULT	6	ALL
OTHERS (WRITE IN)		Q.25

Q.25 Was it something which the tour company could have prevented?

	CODE	ROUTE
DEFINITELY	1	
POSSIBLY	2	
PROBABLY NOT	3	ALL
DK	4	Q.26a

Q.26a Did you <u>complain</u> to anybody?

	CODE	ROUTE
YES	1	Q.26b
NO	2	Q.27

IF YES, ASK:

Q.26b To whom did you complain?

		CODE	ROUTE
ON HOLIDAY	TOUR OPERATOR'S REP	1	
	HOTEL MANAGEMENT	2	
	OTHERS	3	
ON RETURN	TOUR OPERATOR	4	
	TRAVEL AGENT	5	
	ABTA	6	
	OTHERS	7	ALL
	DK	8	Q.26c

Q.26c How satisfied were you with the outcome of your complaint? Were you:

	CODE	ROUTE
SATISFIED	1	
NOT SATISFIED	2	ALL
DK	3	Q.27

Q.27 Considering what it cost, would you say your holiday was **(READ OUT)**

	CODE	ROUTE
VERY GOOD VALUE	1	
FAIRLY GOOD VALUE	2	
NOT VERY GOOD VALUE	3	
POOR VALUE	4	ALL
DK	5	Q.28

Q.28 Would you go on that particular holiday again?

	CODE	ROUTE
DEFINITELY	1	
POSSIBLY	2	
NO	3	ALL
DK	4	Q.29

Q.29 Now, taking <u>everything</u> into account, how satisfied or dissatisfied were you with your holiday? **(SHOW CARD)**

	CODE	ROUTE
TOTALLY SATISFIED	1	CLASS
SATISFIED	2	CLASS
NEITHER SATISFIED NOR DISSATISFIED	3	Q.30
DISSATISFIED	4	Q.30
TOTALLY DISSATISFIED	5	Q.30
DK	6	Q.30

IF NOT "TOTALLY SATISFIED" OR "SATISFIED", ASK:

Q.30 What was the <u>main</u> thing that caused you to be less than satisfied with your holiday?

	CODE	ROUTE
		ALL
		CLASS

Figure 14 Extract from ABTA survey

52

enable examples and lists of answers, known as 'prompts', to be shown to respondents. (There is an example of a prompt card used in the ABTA survey in Figure 14.)

● ●

CASE STUDY: Association of British Travel Agents (ABTA)

The survey conducted by Donald Osborne Research Ltd. for ABTA consisted of 924 personal interviews carried out at 100 locations in Great Britain, using a limited quota sample based on age and sex (see 'Sampling the market' on pages 80–88).

A total of 30 questions, some divided into subsections (see Figure 14) were asked, together with questions to find personal details about the respondent. As Figure 14 shows, the questionnaire contains a number of instructions to the interviewer to control the interviews and ensure standardisation.

The 'ROUTE' instructions by each question tell the interviewer which questions to ask next.

For example, irrespective of the answer they give to Q28, all respondents are asked Q29, but those giving answers 1 or 2 to Q29 ('TOTALLY SATISFIED' OR 'SATISFIED') are not asked Q30. Instead they are asked the classification questions (about age, sex and occupation) straightaway. Only those giving answers 3 to 6 are asked Q30 before they too are classified.

To prompt answers to Q29, respondents are shown a card listing the options open to them. The interviewer is reminded to show the respondents this prompt card when asking the question.

● ●

Telephone interviews

These are much the same as personal interviews, although they allow more interviews to be conducted in the same time, especially when compared with house-to-house surveys. Telephone interviews are particularly cost-effective when the respondents are dispersed over a large geographical area. By definition, only telephone users listed in telephone directories are surveyed and this may limit how representative the sample is, as some groups may be less likely to have a telephone than others. Data can be input directly into computers (Computer Aided Telephone Interviewing or CATI) which makes this the fastest form of both consumer and business research.

ACTIVITY

38

/

2 mins

Can you think of two or three factors that might influence a decision to choose between personal and telephone interview methods?

Compare your thoughts with ours on page 132.

Postal questionnaires

Postal questionnaires are intended to be returned, by respondents, by post. They can be posted out to respondents, included in newspapers, magazines or in the packaging of products, or handed out during personal contacts. Their return rate (the percentage posted back) can vary enormously; to have all returned would be remarkable! Specialist surveys, particularly of business respondents, or where there is a financial incentive to participate, can push responses above 50 per cent. Otherwise, between 10 and 25 per cent would be considered quite normal.

Nevertheless, postal surveys are fairly cheap to conduct, and can be effective where simple, unambiguous questions are involved, and where no control over the order of answering questions is required. (You can't stop people reading right through before they answer the first question.)

ACTIVITY

39

Can you think of a couple of reasons why answers to postal questionnaires might be less reliable than answers to a telephone interview?

Compare your answer with ours on page 132.

3 mins

Hall tests

Traditionally conducted in church halls, these tests can be held anywhere, including trailers specially equipped for previewing advertising. The purpose of the hall test is to allow respondents to experience a product or a promotional campaign and to be interviewed to determine their reaction as they do so. This reduces the risks of launching unsatisfactory new products, or having promotional campaigns which are ineffective.

. . . to allow respondents to experience the product and to be interviewed as they do so . . .

Consumer panels

Many agencies rely on a sample of individuals or households for regular research into consumption patterns and for new product testing. Panel members are recruited to fit a particular membership profile for a fixed period or on an open ended basis. (You will find out more about some of the characteristics which are used in such 'membership profiles' in the section on consumer classification on pages 71–80).

Members may be asked to keep a diary of their consumption, television viewing or other activities. They may also be used for testing new products or assessing reactions to new promotional strategies.

Members may be asked to keep a diary of their consumption

CASE STUDY: Breakfast cereal

A few years ago a manufacturer of an instant breakfast cereal developed new fruit-flavoured versions of its already successful product. Its regular agency, Market Information Services, was asked to test these with its consumer panel. Each household was asked to try the different flavours and the panel member (usually the wife/mother in the family) filled in a postal questionnaire on her family's reaction.

One panel member wrote 'The children wouldn't eat it so I gave it to the dog. The dog was sick'. Needless to say, the company dropped the new product in that particular form!

ACTIVITY

40

5 mins

Why might an agency choose to use a hall test rather than its consumer panel for testing a new product?

Compare your answer with ours on page 132.

Audits

Audits, particularly retail audits, are an ideal way of taking a 'snapshot' of marketing activity at a particular point in time by observing or measuring actual events. Nielson Marketing Research, for example, are one of the most well-known companies in this field, analysing the display footage (amount of shelf space for products) and stock levels of products, their price and promotional activities in representative retail outlets. Like a financial audit, the counting of stock or shelf space, the recording of prices and promotions can indicate to sponsors of such research how they and their competitors are performing in the marketplace.

The Department of Employment Retail Price Index (RPI) relies on a monthly survey of the prices of a list of products and services using an audit approach. (The list itself is the product of information from the diaries of a very large consumer panel.) The Top Forty, used by the BBC, relies on an audit of sales of records in selected record retailers, conducted electronically by Gallup.

ACTIVITY

41

5 mins

Why might a firm be interested in the amount of shelf space allocated to its competitors' products in retailers?

Compare your answer with ours on page 133.

Observation

This can include a form of audit, counting people using a product (e.g. going into a rival's shops), using two-way mirrors or hidden cameras to observe consumer behaviour (e.g. eye movements when looking at retail displays), or to observe interviews or discussion panels (see 'qualitative research' below).

Most of the techniques outlined above rely on the collection of quantitative data. Because we can't collect information from every single person who uses a product, we have to assume that the behaviour of a whole population can be inferred from a 'sample' drawn from it. As we will see in the section 'Sampling the market', the choice of the sample and its size, in order for it to be representative of the population has to be carefully controlled to make it *statistically valid*.

Qualitative research

Qualitative research, also known as 'depth research' or 'motivation research' or 'focus groups', rarely relies on samples large enough to be statistically valid. Instead it relies on the quality of the data gathered, going far beyond the superficial question-and-answer methods of quantitative research. The most commonly used strategy is the one-to-one or small group structured interview or discussion. This does not involve formal interview schedules but relies on the interviewer's skill at directing the discussion and identifying deep-seated attitudes and feelings.

ACTIVITY

42

Using hidden video cameras focused on consumers' reaction to shelf displays, you discover that shoppers look longer at your packaging than at your competitors'.

Your first reaction is to feel pleased that your product is attracting attention. Then your research executive suggests setting up some interviews to determine why this is.

2 mins

Can you think of any reasons why the research executive has proposed this step?

Check your ideas against ours on page 133.

●●

CASE STUDY: Strand Cigarettes

Strand cigarettes are notorious in the advertising industry as an example of the importance of understanding consumer reactions. The product was advertised using a very evocative scene of a man walking along the deserted Strand in London late at night and pausing under a street lamp to light a cigarette. The slogan, which was used at the end, said simply 'You're never alone with a Strand'.

Despite achieving a very high recognition in surveys (many people can still remember it vividly today) the sales plummeted. Subsequent qualitative research revealed that many viewers equated the cigarette with loneliness and despair – the very images used in the advert.

●●

The example of Strand cigarettes shows why the application of qualitative techniques to advertising research has become increasingly common as advertisers attempt to discover what *subliminal message* (a hidden, usually unintended, message) is being carried in their advertisements *before* they use them.

In this section we have looked at a whole range of research designs, and you have found out something about their strengths and weaknesses. In the next section we will focus on those designs which rely on formal questionnaires or interview schedules, and discuss the types of questions which can be used, and how questionnaires and interview schedules are constructed.

Figure 15 Market research designs: a summary

1 Personal interview	Most commonly used. Allows interviewers control and use of prompt cards. More expensive than telephone interviewing, even with modified sampling methods. Can include interviewer assessment (e.g. housing types).
2 Telephone interview	Increasingly used as telephone ownership extended. Frequently used for business surveys or other dispersed specialist populations. Less interviewer control than personal interviewing, but much lower interview cost. Only verbal prompting. Quicker to complete than personal interviewing (particularly with CATI). Excludes all non-telephone and unlisted telephone households.
3 Postal questionnaire	Mostly used where personal and telephone interviewing inappropriate. Variable return rates, highest with specialist populations and/or with incentive to participate. Little control of responses (e.g. group rather than individual completion). Requires fairly simple questions and short questionnaires. Generally less valid than interview designs.
4 Hall tests	Primary purpose is for product or promotion testing. Allows for simulation of various situations. Cost varies according to nature, but more expensive than ordinary personal interviewing. Usually requires quota sampling. Also used with qualitative research design.
5 Consumer panel	Permanent panel, available for testing as with hall tests and for longitudinal studies (over a period of time). Easy to use once established (can be cheaper than hall tests) but continuous involvement may make the panel unrepresentative as they get used to participating. Panel members sometimes paid retainer fees, but will still be cheaper to use than methods relying on sampling.
6 Audit	Valuable for collecting accurate data on pricing, display and promotion activity and for making comparisons over time. Also to assess competitors' performance in the market using display and stock levels as indicators of sales. A labour intensive activity, but often relies on there being a large market for results (see Omnibus Surveys).
7 Observation	Very often used in conjunction with (qualitative) group discussions to help understand consumer behaviour. Extensively used in packaging research to assess consumer reaction (eye-appeal), although this needs to be associated with other indicators of consumer responses. Expensive to operate; requires both equipment and specialist monitoring staff.
8 Qualitative	Can be used in conjunction with 4, 5 and 7. Usually relies on structured discussion, without interview schedules, conducted by specialist staff (usually trained psychologists). Ideal for identifying underlying attitudes and motivations, but lacks statistical validity; generally results from each discussion will not be replicated by the next. Some clients are less influenced by such research as a result, others rely heavily on it.

Questionnaire design

As we have seen, market researchers can use personal or telephone interviews or questionnaires to gather information. When conducting interviews the list of questions are called *interview schedules*, whereas when they are self-administered they are called *questionnaires*. Perhaps the most important distinction is that with self-administered questionnaires, unlike interview schedules, there is no one to control the process or to 'probe' or 'prompt' in a controlled way. (We will come across these two words again later in this section.) For simplicity we will refer to both types here as 'questionnaires'.

In this section we will look at:

● the design of individual questions;
● the design of the whole questionnaire.

You will find out about the main types of question, and the principles which apply in putting them together into a final document.

Types of questions

ACTIVITY

43

➔←

2 mins

Look at these two questions:

a) *'Are you married?'*

b) *'What are your opinions about the development of alternative sources of electricity?'*

What important difference is there between these two questions, in terms of the expected answers the questions might receive?

There is only a choice between 'yes' or 'no' to the first question. For the second question the range of possible answers is enormous. This illustrates the way that we can divide up questions into two main groups:

● those with a limited range of (known) answers;
● those with an unlimited range of answers.

When using these in questionnaire design, the first group enables us to construct a particular type of question known as *closed* questions; the second are *open* questions. The difference between these two is that the answers to closed questions must fit into a limited list of answers. Closed questions are not necessarily simple ones, however; as we will see later, there are types of 'scaling' questions which can obtain some very complex information.

Figure 16 gives examples of closed questions taken from the National Survey of Buying conducted by the British Market Research Bureau for their Target Group Index. You will notice that when listing brand options, the 'OTHER BRANDS' category is used to avoid having to include an exhaustive list of every brand of tinned soup.

It's not absolutely necessary to use closed questions when answers are predictable. If we are trying to measure recall, it's quite possible to use open-ended questions which don't prompt respondents to

FROZEN FISH FINGERS

1. Do you ever serve them? Yes **6** ◯ 1 No ◯ 2

IF YOU DO

2. About how many fish fingers do you serve each WEEK on average?

SIXTEEN or more	◯ 3
ELEVEN to FIFTEEN	◯ 4
NINE or TEN	◯ 5
SEVEN or EIGHT	◯ 6
FIVE or SIX	◯ 7
THREE or FOUR	◯ 8
TWO or less	◯ 9

3. Which brands do you serve?

	Most Often	Others
Bejam	**7** ◯ y	**8** ◯ y
Birds Eye	◯ x	◯ x
Co-op	◯ 0	◯ 0
Findus	◯ 1	◯ 1
Presto	◯ 2	◯ 2
Ross	◯ 3	◯ 3
Sainsburys	◯ 4	◯ 4
Tesco	◯ 5	◯ 5
OTHER BRANDS	◯ 9	◯ 9

OTHER FROZEN FISH/FISH PRODUCTS

1. Do you ever serve it? Yes **9** ◯ 1 No ◯ 2

IF YOU DO

2. About how many portions do you serve each WEEK on average?

FIVE or more	◯ 3
FOUR	◯ 4
THREE	◯ 5
TWO	◯ 6
ONE or less	◯ 7

3. Which brands do you serve?

	Most Often	Others
Bejam	**10** ◯ y	**11** ◯ y
Birds Eye	◯ x	◯ x
Campbells	◯ 0	◯ 0
Co-op	◯ 1	◯ 1
Findus	◯ 2	◯ 2
King Frost	◯ 3	◯ 3
MacFisheries	◯ 4	◯ 4
Presto	◯ 5	◯ 5
Ross	◯ 6	◯ 6
Sainsburys	◯ 7	◯ 7
St. Michael/M & S	◯ 8	◯ 8
Tesco	◯ 9	◯ 9
Ungers	**12** ◯ y	**13** ◯ y
Youngs	◯ x	◯ x
OTHER BRANDS	◯ 9	◯ 9

PACKETED SPAGHETTI, MACARONI & OTHER PASTA (not tinned)

1. Do you ever serve it? Yes **14** ◯ 1 No ◯ 2

IF YOU DO

2. About how many portions do you serve each WEEK on average?

FIVE or more	◯ 3
FOUR	◯ 4
THREE	◯ 5
TWO	◯ 6
ONE	◯ 7
Less than one	◯ 8

3. Which brands do you serve?

	Most Often	Others
Buitoni	**15** ◯ y	**16** ◯ y
Cirio	◯ x	◯ x
Batchelors Super Noodles	◯ 0	◯ 0
Lily Brand	◯ 1	◯ 1
Marshalls	◯ 2	◯ 2
Presto	◯ 3	◯ 3
Quaker Quick	◯ 4	◯ 4
Rakusens	◯ 5	◯ 5
Record	◯ 6	◯ 6
Sainsburys	◯ 7	◯ 7
Tesco	◯ 8	◯ 8
Vesta	◯ 9	◯ 9
OTHER BRANDS	**17** ◯ 9	**18** ◯ 9

TINNED PASTA – INCLUDING SPAGHETTI, RAVIOLI, ETC.

1. Do you ever serve it? Yes **19** ◯ 1 No ◯ 2

IF YOU DO

2. About how many portions do you serve each WEEK on average?

FIVE or more	◯ 3
FOUR	◯ 4
THREE	◯ 5
TWO	◯ 6
ONE	◯ 7
Less than one	◯ 8

3. Which brands do you serve?

	Most Often	Others
Buitoni Ravioli	**20** ◯ y	**21** ◯ y
Crosse & Blackwell:		
Spaghetti Rings	◯ x	◯ x
Spaghetti	◯ 0	◯ 0
Alphabetti Spaghetti	◯ 1	◯ 1
Any other C & B	◯ 2	◯ 2
Heinz:		
Haunted House	◯ 3	◯ 3
Invaders	◯ 4	◯ 4
Macaroni Cheese	◯ 5	◯ 5
Noodle Doodles	◯ 6	◯ 6
Ravioli	◯ 7	◯ 7
Spaghetti Bolognese	◯ 8	◯ 8
Spaghetti Hoops	◯ 9	◯ 9
Spaghetti	**22** ◯ y	**23** ◯ y
Any other Heinz	◯ x	◯ x
Presto	◯ 0	◯ 0
Sainsburys	◯ 1	◯ 1
Tesco	◯ 2	◯ 2
OTHER BRANDS	◯ 9	◯ 9

PACKET SOUP

1. Do you ever serve it? Yes **24** ◯ 1 No ◯ 2

IF YOU DO

2. About how many portions do you serve each WEEK on average?

SIX or more	◯ 3
FIVE	◯ 4
FOUR	◯ 5
THREE	◯ 6
TWO	◯ 7
ONE or less	◯ 8

3. Which brands do you serve?

	Most Often	Others
Batchelors:		
Cup–a–Soup	**25** ◯ y	**26** ◯ y
Slim–a–Soup	◯ x	◯ x
Batchelors Standard	◯ 0	◯ 0
Crosse & Blackwell:		
In boxes	◯ 1	◯ 1
Instant Soup	◯ 2	◯ 2
Heinz Soupermug	◯ 3	◯ 3
Knorr Quick Soup	◯ 4	◯ 4
Knorr Hearty Soup	◯ 5	◯ 5
Other Knorr	◯ 6	◯ 6
Maggi	◯ 7	◯ 7
Presto	◯ 8	◯ 8
Sainsburys	◯ 9	◯ 9
St. Michael/M & S	**27** ◯ y	**28** ◯ y
OTHER BRANDS	◯ 9	◯ 9

TINNED SOUP

1. Do you ever serve it? Yes **29** ◯ 1 No ◯ 2

IF YOU DO

2. About how many portions do you serve each WEEK on average?

SEVEN or more	◯ 3
FIVE or SIX	◯ 4
FOUR	◯ 5
THREE	◯ 6
TWO	◯ 7
ONE or less	◯ 8

3. Which brands do you serve?

	Most Often	Others
Baxters	**30** ◯ y	**31** ◯ y
Campbells:		
Condensed	◯ x	◯ x
Main Course	◯ 0	◯ 0
Bumper Harvest	◯ 1	◯ 1
Co–op	◯ 2	◯ 2
Crosse & Blackwell:		
Waistline	◯ 3	◯ 3
Standard	◯ 4	◯ 4
Fine Fare	◯ 5	◯ 5
Heinz Big Soup	◯ 6	◯ 6
Heinz Classic	◯ 7	◯ 7
Heinz Standard	◯ 8	◯ 8
Presto	◯ 9	◯ 9
Sainsburys	**32** ◯ y	**33** ◯ y
Tesco	◯ x	◯ x
Weight Watchers	◯ 0	◯ 0
OTHER BRANDS	◯ 9	◯ 9

PLEASE USE PENCIL ONLY

002021/004/120
FRONT/01

SR4700187

Figure 16

60

self-administered questionnaires into giving specific answers. In this case, interviewers will need to 'code' the answers afterwards. This means identifying and grouping commonly used answers in such a way that they can be counted for analysis purposes.

Activity 44 gives you an opportunity to work out standard responses which have the effect of closing a question.

ACTIVITY

44

5 mins

Below is a list of twelve responses to the question: 'How often do you go to the cinema?' See if you can write a standard set of four or five answers to this question which would include all those listed here.

- *'Every week.'*
- *'It must be two or three years since I last went.'*
- *'Most Saturdays.'*
- *'I usually take the kids during their school holidays.'*
- *'Quite regularly; I suppose about 2 or 3 times a month.'*
- *'Never!'*
- *'I went last summer' (it's now spring).*
- *'I should think it's more than 10 years since I last went'.*
- *'Once or twice a month.'*
- *'Every few months, I suppose.'*
- *'I went last week for the first time in years.'*
- *'About once a fortnight.'*

Figure 17 shows three possible closed question designs for obtaining the information illustrated in Activity 44. The first example, 17(a), is one possible way of grouping the twelve responses to the question 'How often do you go to the cinema?' Was your answer similar to this?

In the other two examples you will find alternative versions of the question; these are likely to give far more accurate information than the original question. 17(b) asks respondents to count their attendances rather than make estimates, as in 17(a). Neither will be perfectly accurate, but 17(b) will give a more precise picture.

The question in 17(c) is a way of understanding cinema-goers' perceptions of themselves. This is useful in designing promotion strategies and in understanding customer behaviour. Questions 17(b) and 17(c) could, quite usefully, both be used to relate actual attendance rates to customers' perceptions.

Open-ended questions are most commonly used in practice in initial questionnaire design using small test samples to identify how effective particular questions are in eliciting information, to discover problems of understanding or ambiguity, and to identify likely responses which could be used in closed question design.

a) 'How often do you go to the cinema?'	Once a fortnight or more Once a month Once or twice every three months Less often than above Never (in last 2 years)
b) 'How many times have you been to the cinema in the last 12 months?'	At least 20 times Between 10 and 19 times Between 5 and 9 times Between 1 and 4 times Not at all
(This question encourages respondents to give a count of cinema attendance in a prescribed period.)	
c) 'How would you describe your cinema attendance?' (SHOW PROMPT CARD)	Frequent Regular Occasional Rare Never
(This question requires respondents to select from a list – on the prompt card – and gives an idea of their perception of themselves as cinema-goers, and their likely interest in cinema.)	

Figure 17 Questions and answers

Where interviewers are involved, answers to closed questions may not be offered to respondents; where they are this is known as prompting. As we have seen, in personal interviews this is often done by showing respondents a card with the answers on – the prompt card.

ACTIVITY

45

In interviews, the respondents aren't usually shown the questionnaire itself. Can you suggest one or two reasons why?

Compare your answer with the one on page 133.

2 mins

In some forms of interview, the inteviewer may be encouraged to 'probe'; this means asking supplementary questions to encourage recall ('Are you sure that's all?' or 'Can you think of any more?') This has to be done very carefully to avoid upsetting respondents and to avoid biasing the responses. The art of interviewing is quite a difficult one and most market research agencies or fieldwork agencies give interviewers training before letting them loose!

(Fieldwork agencies are firms with teams of interviewers who undertake the actual interviewing – fieldwork – on subcontract from the research agency. Some agencies rely on freelance interviewers who are employed directly, often by a number of different MR agencies.)

So far we've treated all closed questions as being much the same; a question for which there are a list of straightforward answers. Most questionnaires rely on this type of question as a source of information but they don't allow us to assess more sensitive issues. After all, people are not machines with precise sets of behaviour or clear-cut ideas.

ACTIVITY

46

10 mins

Look at the following questions; tick the ones which can be answered by choosing either 'yes' or 'no'.

- *'Do you watch the ITN News at Ten?'*
- *'Do you eat Heinz Baked Beans?'*
- *'Do you think all violent criminals should be sent to prison?'*
- *'Do you read a Sunday paper?'*

Can you identify any shortcomings in the information these questions would provide?

Try rewriting one or two of these questions so that a yes/no answer would provide more accurate information.

Compare your answers with ours on page 133.

Scaling questions

Well-phrased questions can make yes/no answers give much more precise information. However there are some issues, to do with people's opinions and attitudes, which cannot be assessed using simple yes/no answers.

For this reason various systems of 'scaling' have been devised to help establish the exact nature of behaviour and attitudes. The four most commonly used (although there are others) are;

- rank order scaling;
- Likert scaling;
- semantic differential scaling;
- forced choice scaling.

We will look at an example of each technique in turn.

You can see examples of these four types of question in Figures 18 (a), (b), (c) and (d). If you look at each of these in turn you will see how each attempts to discover the finer detail of complex aspects of attitudes and behaviour.

a) *Rank order scaling*

Below you will find a list of ten popular makes of car, in alphabetical order; put a number beside each to indicate your order of preference for them. (For example, if you prefer Ford to the others put a '1' in the box, then a '2' for your second favourite, and so on.)

Austin Rover ☐
Fiat ☐
Honda ☐
Nissan ☐
Peugeot Talbot ☐
Renault ☐
Toyota ☐
Vauxhall-Opel ☐
Volkswagen ☐

---

b) *Likert scaling*

Look at the following statements; for each one choose the option which seems to you to be the most accurate by circling the appropriate number.

i) 'Foreign cars are more reliable than British cars.'

Strongly Agree	Agree	Uncertain	Disagree	Strongly Disagree
+2	+1	0	−1	−2

ii) 'Parts for foreign cars are more expensive than for British cars.'

Strongly Agree	Agree	Uncertain	Disagree	Strongly Disagree
+2	+1	0	−1	−2

---

c) *Semantic differential scaling*

Look at the following statement and the pairs of words in the list. Circle the number which most closely reflects how strongly you feel about the choice of words, choosing '0' as neutral, '1' as slightly, '2' as moderately, '3' as strongly.

'Compared with British made cars, foreign cars are:

stylish	3	2	1	0	1	2	3	mundane
expensive	3	2	1	0	1	2	3	inexpensive
long-lived	3	2	1	0	1	2	3	short-lived
rust-free	3	2	1	0	1	2	3	rust-prone

---

d) *Forced choice scaling*

Below is a series of pairs of statements; you should choose the statement in each pair which reflects your own feelings. In each case you should choose the one, even if you don't fully agree with the statement, which you most closely agree with.

  i) 'People who drive British cars are staid and unimaginative.'

or

   'People who drive British cars are looking for a well-built and safe car.'

 ii) 'People who drive foreign cars are flashy.'

or

   'People who drive foreign cars are stylish.'

iii) 'People who drive British cars are looking for a well-built and safe car.'

or

   'People who drive foreign cars are stylish.'

Notice that some of the statements appear more than once. We will explain the reason for that later in this section.

Figure 18 Scaling methods

Fill in your own answers to the four examples in Figure 18. Do the results reveal anything to you about your attitudes to cars which you weren't aware of? If you do this faintly in pencil you can rub out your answers and try the questions on friends to see if their attitudes differ from yours. If they do, can you think why this might be?

The simple rank order scaling technique (Figure 18(a)) is useful for identifying people's perceptions of the relative worth of brands and other choices open to them. What it doesn't do is tell you how great a difference they perceive to exist between these brands. Figure 19 illustrates this; the rank order shown in the left-hand column simply lists brands in order. The relative value of each brand as actually perceived by the respondent is shown alongside.

The respondent's ranking of Brands A–E by questionnaire	The respondent's actual ranking of Brands A–E
1st Brand A	Brand A 1st
2nd Brand B	
3rd Brand C	
4th Brand D	
5th Brand E	
	Brand B 2nd
	Brand C 3rd
	Brand D 4th
	Brand E 5th
An 'ordinal' scale	An 'interval' scale

Figure 19 Rank order scales – ordinal and interval scales

The left-hand list is in order (it's called an ordinal scale) but doesn't say how much more 'A' is preferred to 'B', 'C', etc. The right-hand scale does show this, the intervals between the different brands reflect the differences in preference. In this example, brand A is very much more preferred to brand B than brand B is to brand C. This type of scale is called an interval scale, but although it is more accurate in showing preference it is far more difficult to obtain the information needed to construct one.

The scaling methods shown in Figures 18 (b), (c) and (d) attempt to measure the size of these intervals by giving respondents a chance to show how strong their preferences are for different statements.

Figure 20 contains the results of 100 interviews in which the question in Figure 18(b) about reliability was asked. Follow through the instructions and complete the table. What can you conclude about people's typical attitudes to the reliability of foreign cars?

'Foreign cars are more reliable than British cars.'

Option	(a) Value	(b) Respondents	(c) [(a)×(b)]
Strongly agree	+2	53	+ _____
Agree	+1	34	+ _____
Uncertain	0	8	0 _____
Disagree	−1	4	− _____
Strongly disagree	−2	1	− _____
		= 100	= + _____ (d)

i) Multiply the number in column (a) by the number in column (b) and put the answer in column (c). (Remember $8 \times 0 = 0$.)

ii) Add together the first two numbers with the + signs in column (c) and take away from this the last two numbers with the minus signs. Put your answer in the box (d).

iii) Divide the number in box (d) by 100; put your answer here + .

iv) What does this tell you about people's general attitude to the statement?

Figure 20

Check your answers against the ones on page 134.

As you can see, the Likert scale (illustrated in Figure 18(b)) measures the strength of an attitude or feeling such as agreement/disagreement. The semantic differential (Figure 18(c)) in contrast uses pairs of descriptions or adjectives which are the opposites of each other. By recording the respondents' attitudes through their strength of choice for a word in each pair we begin to measure and build up a detailed picture of that attitude.

You will notice that both the Likert and Semantic scales include a neutral value of '0'; this neutral position is frequently included in this type of scale, but it can be left out.

Why might a market researcher decide to leave out a neutral value in an attitude scale? Write a couple of sentences to explain your reasoning.

Compare your answer with the one on page 134.

2 mins

This questionnaire is part of the 'SPOC/EPOC' (Student Perception/Employer Perception of College) Market Research System developed by the Responsive College Project. It uses both closed and open-ended questions to investigate student's perceptions of the course and the college after 'consumption' (completion of the course).

6 Read each statement in this section carefully.
Please tell us what you think by ticking one box for each statement.

	Very Good	Good	So-So	Below Standard	Bad
The general appearance of the college	☐	☐	☐	☐	☐
The general atmosphere in the college	☐	☐	☐	☐	☐
The teaching on your course	☐	☐	☐	☐	☐
The course content	☐	☐	☐	☐	☐
The organisation of your course	☐	☐	☐	☐	☐

	Very Good	Good	So-So	Below Standard	Bad	Received None
Careers help and advice you received	☐	☐	☐	☐	☐	☐
Personal help and support you received	☐	☐	☐	☐	☐	☐

If you would like to add anything about your college or your course please write it here:

....
....
....
....
....
....
....

Thank you for your help

IF YOU WOULD LIKE INFORMATION ABOUT ANY OTHER COURSES AT THIS COLLEGE PLEASE FILL IN THE DETAILS BELOW:

SUBJECT/SUBJECTS IN WHICH YOU ARE INTERESTED: ....

....

LEVEL: ....

DO YOU WANT TO STUDY PART-TIME ☐   FULL-TIME ☐

DAY-TIME ☐   EVENING ☐

SPOC4   PART OF THE SPOC/EPOC QUALITY MONITORING SYSTEM
The Responsive College Programme, FESC, Coombe Lodge, Blagdon, Bristol BS18 6RG   *QUALITY* ✔

Page 4

Figure 21 A self-completion questionnaire

It is possible to use either five-point or seven-point scales for both types of question. One reason for choosing seven is to allow for the fine shades of opinion; five encourages people to use the extremes which respondents often avoid with seven. Figure 21 shows an example of a five point

Likert scales allow the respondent to express shades of feeling

Likert-type scale contained in a self-completion questionnaire used in many colleges.

The final technique to be discussed is forced choice scaling, which is shown in Figure 18 (d). This enables the ranking of more complex attitudes than the type shown in Figure 18 (a). By combining all possible pairs of a list of statements and forcing respondents in each case to choose one they most agree with, a much more detailed picture of the respondent's attitudes can be built up. The example shown uses a simple 'ordinal' scale, but more complex techniques can be employed to give an 'interval' scale, which measures the relative 'strength' of the statements.

ACTIVITY

50

>←←

5 mins

Look back to the types of survey design listed in Figure 15. In which ones could scaling methods be employed?

Compare your answers with the ones on page 134.

To conclude this section, let's summarise the types of questions we've looked at. These are:

● Open ended questions (where respondents choose their own answers);
● Closed questions (where respondents select their answers from a list of options);
● Scaling questions (closed questions which enable attitudes to be ranked and measured).

We have seen some of the ways that each of these can be used in market research questionnaires. We will now go on to look at the overall design of questionnaires themselves.

Putting the questionnaire together

Choosing a type of question to use and designing the actual questions requires a surprising degree of skill. So too does the task of putting them together in a questionnaire. Respondents' answers can easily be biased by poor design of individual questions, or of the whole questionnaire. In the worst case, they may be so put off that they refuse to answer at all.

... they may be so put off that they refuse to answer at all.

ACTIVITY

51

Try thinking of two or three ways in which poor design could show up in a questionnaire. What effect might these design faults have on the respondents?

Compare your thoughts with ours on page 134.

3 mins

The key to good questionnaire design is to build up gently to the issues you wish to explore, to avoid being difficult to understand (two simple questions rather than one complex one) and, if you want to hide your true interests, add a number of plausible but irrelevant questions as camouflage.

A questionnaire has three main components:

● Introduction
● Respondent classification questions
● Main questions

The *introduction* is designed to explain the purpose of the survey, to stress anonymity and to ask the prospective respondent to agree to participate. This section will normally be pre-written for the interviewer who will learn it by heart before commencing work. If the questionnaire is for self-completion, the introduction will be printed so that it is the first section the respondent will read.

ACTIVITY

52

⟩⟨

3 mins

Why do you think interviewers are not allowed to decide the content of their own introduction?

We have given two reasons for this on page 134.

The *classification of respondents* enables researchers to identify whether they fit the sample which is being surveyed. It also allows researchers to identify how answers to the questions vary according to the type of respondent. We will look at this in much more detail in the next section, on consumer classification.

However, it is important to decide where in the questionnaire the questions which will seek out this information should lie. When a specific sample is being sought (such as 'housewives under 44') it makes sense to ask at the beginning to avoid wasting time. If this isn't the case, the questions are usually left till last, as they are easy to answer and leave the respondent feeling comfortable with the interview process.

. . . easy to answer, and leave the respondent feeling comfortable with the interview process.

The *main body of the questionnaire* contains the range of questions set out using one or more of the styles we have been looking at in this section. In general this section should start with simple, factual questions ('what make and model of car do you drive?') and move on if necessary to more complex ones, such as the various scales for assessing attitudes.

This gradual build-up of the questionnaire from simple ideas to more complex ones helps respondents to clarify their own thoughts as they fill it in. Jumping in at the deep end may well scare people off!

In the next two sections you will be finding out more about consumer classification and about sampling methods. Both these aspects of market research are important in questionnaire design, since to undertake them, the inclusion of appropriate questions in the correct position is necessary. Once you have worked through these sections you will have a clear picture of all the factors which shape the design of questionnaires.

Consumer classification

You have already come across the idea of market segmentation – dividing the total market into groups according to their characteristics – in the first workbook in this series. These characteristics are the basis on which we can also classify respondents in market research (since, after all, that is how the segments of the market are actually identified). There are so many people in the market place that without grouping them together into segments, reflecting common characteristics, it would be impossible to start meeting their individual needs.

ACTIVITY

53

>←

3 mins

Using what you already know about market segmentation from the first workbook in the series, list six key characteristics which could be used to classify respondents to a survey.

Compare your answers with the ones on page 135 before reading on.

We shall look briefly in turn at each of the main consumer classifications which are frequently used in market research.

Age is a fairly obvious factor to use in classification, although it can present problems for analysis. If you think about it, each of a thousand respondents is likely to be a different age. One will be 25 today: another 25 years, one month, and six days! Normally we would group both in the same age category, 25 (to be precise '25 and over, but under 26'), but that is a fairly arbitrary decision. We could choose to use bigger groups, with larger age spans.

Look at the following sets of age groups. Which age group in each set do the two respondents mentioned above fit into? (Circle the appropriate age groups before reading on.)

Set 1	Set 2	Set 3	Set 4
15–19	16–20	15–20	16–25
20–24	21–25	20–25	26–35
25–29	26–30	25–30	36–45
30–34	31–35	30–35	46–55

You will probably have realised that it is easy to find the appropriate age range in sets 1, 2 and 4 (the third, second and first respectively) but in set 3 both our 25 year-olds could be included in two age ranges, the second and third. What you have seen here is an easy pitfall when grouping together such features. The groups provided in set 3 are not exclusive. No respondent should be able to be included in more than one group.

You might also have noticed how changing the grouping puts our two respondents together with different respondents. In particular set 4 lumps together 16 year-olds with twenty-five year-olds. One of the key questions which should be thought about when deciding upon such groups is how similar to each other the people in a chosen age band will be in terms of their consumption behaviour.

Social class is one of the most difficult concepts to use in consumer classification, since it can have so many different meanings. In marketing we try to avoid using phrases like 'upper class', 'middle class' or 'working class' as the meanings people attach to these labels can vary widely. To use social class as a factor, we need some agreed standards.

Figure 22 shows the two social classifications you are most likely to encounter. Each bases the various classes of consumer on a series of objective criteria.

The Registrar-General's classification is used in government statistics, and is often found in social research. It is based on occupations grouped according to social status rather than income.

The JICNARS Social Grading is very similar, being based on employment although using slightly different definitions. As the name suggests, this classification was originally used for readership surveys (of newspapers, periodicals and other magazines) but has become the 'de facto' standard for most social class gradings in market research.

Look at the following job titles. Using the classifications in Figure 22, which social class and social grading do you think each belongs to?

a) Primary school headteacher
b) Secretary
c) Motor vehicle mechanic
d) Bricklayer's mate

Compare your answers with the ones on page 135.

Figure 22 Social class classification

a) JICNARS (Joint Industry Committee for National Readership
Surveys) 'Social Grading on the National Readership Survey'

SOCIAL GRADE	SOCIAL STATUS	OCCUPATION	% OF ADULTS OVER 15, 1986
A	Upper middle class	High managerial, administrative or professional	2.7
B	Middle class	Intermediate managerial, administrative or professional	14.5
Cl	Lower middle class	Supervisory or clerical, managerial, administrative or professional	22.7
C2	Skilled working class	Skilled manual workers	27.6
D	Working class	Semi and unskilled manual workers	17.6
E	Those at lowest level of subsistence	State pensioners or widows (no other earner), casual or lowest-grade workers	14.8

b) Registrar-General's classification of social class

SOCIAL CLASS		EXAMPLE OCCUPATIONS
I	Professional	Doctors, lawyers, chemists, clergy
II	Intermediate occupations	Most managerial and senior administrative posts (including teachers, nurses and MPs).
III	Skilled occupations; (N) Non-manual (M) Manual	Typists, clerical workers, sales representatives Cooks, railway guards, bricklayers, foremen/forewomen in engineering etc.
IV	Partly-skilled occupations	Bar staff, bus conductors, canteen assistants, telephone operators
V	Unskilled occupations	Office cleaners, labourers

Much fuller descriptions are used for coding questionnaires, so sufficient details of a respondent's occupation must be obtained to allow their social class or grade to be determined. Figure 23 shows the questions used by JICNARS to obtain these details.

One problem often encountered is distinguishing between the respondent and his (or more frequently her) household or family for classification purposes. A household is a group of people; to classify the household means lumping together all the individuals into one category.

This procedure obviously ignores the differences in attitudes and behaviour which may exist among the members of the household. Nevertheless it is common to treat the social grading of all members of the household as being set by one person. This is done by using the occupation of the 'head of the household'; for a married couple (with or without children) this is normally assumed to be the husband.

CLASSIFICATION DATA (ii) (cont.) – HOUSEHOLD RELATED

EMPLOYMENT CODE OF HOH (i.e. person coded 5 under Household Status).
HEAD OF HOUSEHOLD IS –

FULL-TIME EMPLOYED 7
PART-TIME EMPLOYED/UNEMPLOYED/SICK/RETIRED/WIDOWED/PENSIONER
 With income from all sources (salary, private means, private pension, disablement pension,
 compensation, etc) coming to £......... *(£42 Single/£66 Married) a week or over* .. 8
PART-TIME EMPLOYED/UNEMPLOYED/SICK/RETIRED/WIDOWED/PENSIONER
 With income from all above sources coming to less than £ .... *(£42 Single/£66 Married) a week* 9

---

*IF EMPLOYMENT CODE 7 OR 8 IS RINGED
OR IF THERE IS NO CHIEF WAGE EARNER
THE OCCUPATION DETAILS RELATE TO THE
HEAD OF HOUSEHOLD (Record at A below)*

*IF EMPLOYMENT CODE 9 IS RINGED THE
OCCUPATION DETAILS RELATE TO CHIEF
WAGE FARNER (Record at A below)*

*IF H H EMPLOYMENT CODE 9 IS
RINGED CHECK BACK WITH
HOUSEHOLD COMPOSITION GRID
FOR THE CHIEF WAGE EARNER*

RING 'CWE' CODE AGAINST
APPROPRIATE PERSON IN
GRID ON PAGE 21

CLASSIFICATION DATA (ii) INFORMANT RELATED

ASK ALL		(24)S
CD.8 At what age did you finish your full-time education	14 or under	Y
	15	X
	16	0
	17	1
	18	2
	19	3
	20	4
	21-23	5
	24 or over	6
	Still studying	7
	O.U.O.	8

RECORD INFORMANT'S OCCUPATION
DETAILS AT B. BELOW. (IF INFORMANT
IS HOH OR CWE AND THEREFORE
RECORDED AT A, STATE)

OCCUPATION DETAILS (See manual)	A. Head of Household or Chief Wage Earner	B. Informant
What type of firm or organisation does/did (this person) work for? STATE (a) Type of firm etc (including what the firm makes/does etc)		
(b) Name of firm/organisation		
What job does/did (this person) actually do?		
IF IN CIVIL SERVICE, FORCES, POLICE, ETC. What is his/her rank or grade?		
IF OTHER Does/did (this person) hold any particular position in the organisation? STATE (e.g. foreman, typing supervisor, office manager, company secretary, etc) IF SELF-EMPLOYED STATE THIS.		

IF PROPRIETOR OF BUSINESS OR A MANAGER OR SUPERVISOR (i.e. RESPONSIBLE FOR THE WORK OF OTHER PEOPLE)	(a) Total at this place INCLUDE THIS PERSON & STATE No. IN ALL CASES	(b) No. for whom responsible STATE No.	(a) Total at this place INCLUDE THIS PERSON & STATE No. IN ALL CASES	(b) No. for whom responsible STATE No.
(a) Roughly how many people work at the place where (this person) works INCLUDE THIS PERSON. ENTER ACTUAL NUMBER IF POSSIBLE, OR NEAREST APPROXIMATION	200+	200+	200+	200+
	25-199	25-199	25-199	25-199
	10-24	10-24	10-24	10-24
(b) For how many is he/she responsible?	less than 10	less than 10	less than 10	less than 10

ASK FOR ALL Has (this person) any qualifications? (such as apprenticeships, professional qualifications, university degrees, diplomas etc.) STATE WHAT QUALIFICATIONS HELD		

(31)S			(32)M	IF INFORMANT IS HOH/CWE OR WIFE OF HOH/CWE ASK		(33)S
SOCIAL GRADE *OF HEAD OF HOUSE HOLD OR CHIEF WAGE EARNER ·*	A	Y			£1,930	0
	B	X		**NET INCOME OF HOH OR CWE***SHOW INCOME CARD*	£2,415	1
	C1	0			£3,015	2
	C2	1			£3,770	3
	D	2		Which of these comes	£4,710	4
	E	3		closest to your (his/her) income,	£5,890	5
				that is after, deducting	£7,360	6
			(34)M	income tax, national	£9,205	7
	O.U.O.	X		insurance,	£11,505	8
	O.U.O.	0		pension schemes	£14,380	9
				and so on?	£17,975	X
	O.U.O. (SG/HOH)	4			**£22,470 or more**	Y
	O.U.O. (SG/CWE)	5				(47)S
					Refused	X
					O.U.O.	Y

OFFICE USE ONLY					
SOCIAL GRADE		(41)S	**EMPLOYMENT STATUS OF INFORMANT**		(43)S
OF INFORMANT	A	Y			
	B	X			
	C1	0	Self-employed		
	C2	1	25+ employees,		Y
	D	2	1 –24 employees		X
	E	3	No employees		0
INFORMANT HAS CHILDREN		(22)M	Employer		
0-23 months		3	Manager 25+		1
2-4 years		4	1 -24		2
5-10 years		5	Foreman manual		3
11-15 years		2	Non-Manual		4
16-20 years		6	Apprentice		5
21+ years		7	Not elsewhere classified		7
Don't know/not stated		8			
No children		9	Not applicable		8
			Refused		9

OCCUPATION CODE				S I C		(76)S
(35)S	(36)S	(37)M	(38)S	(39)S	(40)S	

Space to (76) JN(77 80)

Figure 23 Extract from National Readership Survey

To classify the household means lumping together all the individuals into one category

---

ACTIVITY

56

What reason do you think there is for relying solely on the husband's occupation to classify a household, now that in a majority of married couples both partners go to work?

2–3 mins

Compare your thoughts with ours on page 135.

One final point to note is that recently unemployed people and retired people with occupational pensions (in addition to state 'old age' pensions) are classified by their previous occupation. It has been found that their consumer behaviour does not change significantly from when they were employed. However, long-term unemployed and those dependent on state pensions or other benefits are classified in group 'E'.

Employment may also be used as a characteristic (apart from social grading purposes) where particular occupational areas are being investigated. This would be useful in researching products (e.g. supplies of industrial protective clothing) which are work-related. Different patterns of employment (full-time, part-time, self-employment) may also be used where relevant.

Education can also be a separate factor for classification purposes. When included, educational characteristics are usually recorded in terms of numbers of years post-compulsory (i.e. post-16) education, or the highest level of qualification obtained.

ACTIVITY

57

Which of the following organisations might be interested in classification of respondents based on specific employment and/or educational characteristics?

a) The publisher of a weekly magazine on corporate finance
b) A sock manufacturer
c) Macmillan Education Ltd (who publish this text)

3 mins

Compare your answers with the ones on page 135.

Marital status and family size are factors which can be of great value in understanding patterns of consumption; both will influence lifestyle and the amount of money people have available to spend on different products (known as 'disposable income'). For example, products may be designed primarily either for single or married men (or women); some for small or large families (how many single men or women will buy two or four pint containers of milk from supermarkets? how many families of six will buy toilet rolls singly?).

Housing type and housing tenancy can be of interest to suppliers of particular products – for example, Everest Double Glazing is likely to be of little interest to the owner of a new luxury house, or to the tenant of rented property. On the other hand, identifying the owner-occupier of a detached period property may well mean identifying the ideal client for double-glazing (or for Rentokil's timber preservation treatments!)

Location is a geographical factor that can be used to identify certain consumption patterns. These differences may be a reflection of cultural differences around the country, or of the difference between urban, suburban, country, town or rural environments. Once again, such characteristics may be of limited interest to some organisations, but to others they could be major determinants of consumption patterns.

ACTIVITY

58

Figure 24 shows the usage patterns of buses ('Have you made any bus journeys in the last seven days?') analysed by residential location. What location factors seem to be important in determining usage?

10 mins

Compare your answer with the one on page 135.

| Residential location | Have you made any bus journeys in the last seven days? | | | | Total |
| | Yes | | No | | |
	Number	%	Number	%	Number
Urban, large conurbation	140	63.6	80	36.4	220
Suburban, large conurbation	216	72.0	84	28.0	300
Other urban	105	52.5	95	47.5	200
Other suburban	61	24.4	189	75.6	150
Small town	32	21.3	118	78.7	150
Rural, village	16	16.0	84	84.0	100

Figure 24 Analysis by residential location

Race, religion and political affiliation are factors which can present difficulties to researchers but can be of some significance, particularly in opinion polling and social research. The difficulties often arise in the wording of questions and the way that possible choice of answers may have different meanings for the interviewer and the respondent. For example 'What race do you belong to?' invites the answer 'The human race'. Limiting answers to a choice between, say black and white, may cause problems for people of Indian or Chinese origin, not to mention those of mixed race.

Similar problems can occur over religion (responding 'C of E' doesn't mean people actually go to church) and in political affiliation. (Does a Conservative have to be a party member, a consistent Tory voter, or merely to have voted Tory at the last election?)

Even more importantly questions on race, religion or political affiliation may be regarded as intrusive or provocative by the respondent, and cause them to reject the questionnaire as a whole.

All the characteristics listed above (and many others) are used to classify respondents because it is believed that they can be used to identify coherent groups in the population who behave in a particular (and predictable) way, or who will be influenced in the same way by particular stimuli.

The difficulty for most organisations is that it is usually a combination of these characteristics which shapes consumer behaviour – not just age, but also social class, housing type, family size, etc. For this reason multi-faceted *lifestyle* concepts have been developed.

Lifestyles are well illustrated in the favourite stereotypes of the 'Yuppies' (young, upwardly-mobile professionals) and 'Dinkies' (double income, no kids). Popular though these images have become, they are based on rather superficial ideas, and other more valid classifications have been developed. Figure 25 illustrates one system, known as SAGACITY.

THE SAGACITY LIFE CYCLE GROUPINGS

The basic thesis of the SAGACITY grouping is that people have different aspirations and behaviour patterns as they go through their life cycle. Four main stages of life cycle are defined which are sub-divided by income and occupation groups:

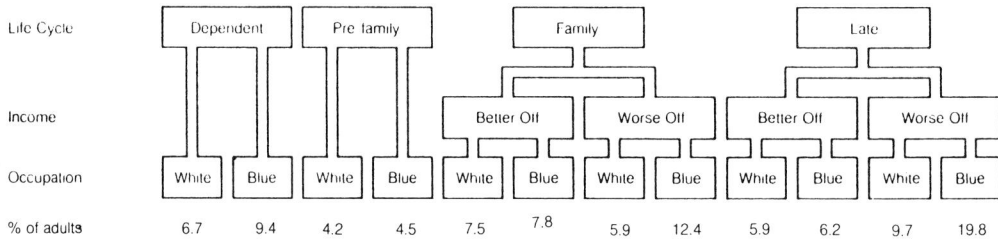

Life Cycle	Dependent		Pre family		Family				Late			
Income					Better Off		Worse Off		Better Off		Worse Off	
Occupation	White	Blue	White	Blue	White	Blue	White	Blue	White	Blue	White	Blue
% of adults	6.7	9.4	4.2	4.5	7.5	7.8	5.9	12.4	5.9	6.2	9.7	19.8

Definitions of life cycle stages
Dependent — Mainly under 24s, living at home or full-time student.
Pre-family — Under 35s, who have established their own household but have no children.
Family — Housewives and heads of household, under 65, with one or more children in the household.
Late — Includes all adults whose children have left home or who are over 35 and childless.

Definitions of occupation groups
White — Head of household is in the ABC1 occupation group.
Blue — Head of household is in the C2DE occupation group.

Figure 25 The SAGACITY life cycle groupings

ACTIVITY
59
>←
5 mins

Pick three or four people you know well, of fairly different ages and in different occupations. Which SAGACITY group does each belong to (i.e. which of the small boxes on the bottom row of Figure 25 do they best fit)? Is there an obvious difference in their consumption behaviour (e.g. type of car, favourite drinks, holiday patterns, etc.)?

Geodemographics is a second approach to multi-factor classification of individuals. Geodemographic techniques link where people live to their age, family type, race and employment (through the data gathered from the Census), and postcodes are used to identify residential location. This means that by sampling from particular areas a researcher can predict the particular category of respondent. From this information it is then possible to promote products to those people that the research has identified as the likeliest consumers. This can be done for example by using selective direct mail.

The most frequently used geodemographic classification is the ACORN system, shown in Figure 26, which classifies areas according to housing type, in two tiers of increasing detail.

ACTIVITY
60
>←
5 mins

Think about the area you live in. Try allocating it to an appropriate ACORN group and type.

Repeat the process with one or two other locations you know well. If you get the chance, compare your classifications with those of a colleague rating the same locations.

```
A C O R N   P R O F I L E   R E P O R T
=========================================
A Company
AREA : GB ACORN Profile
BASE : ALL G.B.                            ----- 1987 population  -----
                                           1987 pop   %   BASE %  INDEX
        ACORN Groups
A   Agricultural Areas                     1870387   3.5    3.5    100
B   Modern Family Housing, Higher Incomes  9240962  17.1   17.1    100
C   Older Housing of Intermediate Status   9622087  17.8   17.8    100
D   Older Terraced Housing                 2309623   4.3    4.3    100
E   Council Estates - Category I           7046273  13.0   13.0    100
F   Council Estates - Category II          4844799   9.0    9.0    100
G   Council Estates - Category III         3867644   7.2    7.2    100
H   Mixed Inner Metropolitan Areas         2080276   3.8    3.8    100
I   High Status Non-family Areas           2268742   4.2    4.2    100
J   Affluent Suburban Housing              8577830  15.9   15.9    100
K   Better-off Retirement Areas            2064291   3.8    3.8    100

        ACORN Types
A1  Agricultural Villages                  1431922   2.6    2.6    100
A2  Areas of Farms and Smallholdings        438465   0.8    0.8    100
B3  Post-war Functional Private Housing    2313416   4.3    4.3    100
B4  Modern Private Housing, Young Families  1870727   3.5    3.5    100
B5  Established Private Family Housing      3206083   5.9    5.9    100
B6  New Detached Houses, Young Families    1511279   2.8    2.8    100
B7  Military Bases                          339457   0.6    0.6    100
C8  Mixed Owner-occupied and Council Estates 1885816  3.5    3.5    100
C9  Small Town Centres and Flats above Shops 2211957  4.1    4.1    100
C10 Villages with Non-farm Employment      2571793   4.8    4.8    100
C11 Older Private Housing, Skilled Workers 2952521   5.5    5.5    100
D12 Unmodernised Terraces, Older People    1353182   2.5    2.5    100
D13 Older Terraces, Lower Income Families   748562   1.4    1.4    100
D14 Tenement Flats Lacking Amenities        207879   0.4    0.4    100
E15 Council Estates, Well-off Older Workers 1868836   3.5    3.5    100
E16 Recent Council Estates                 1487727   2.8    2.8    100
E17 Better Council Estates, Younger Workers 2661338   4.9    4.9    100
E18 Small Council Houses, often Scottish   1028372   1.9    1.9    100
F19 Low Rise Estates in Industrial Towns   2485780   4.6    4.6    100
F20 Inter-war Council Estates, Older People 1586035   2.9    2.9    100
F21 Council Housing, Elderly People         772984   1.4    1.4    100
G22 New Council Estates in Inner Cities    1073155   2.0    2.0    100
G23 Overspill Estates, Higher Unemployment 1646156   3.0    3.0    100
G24 Council Estates with Some Overcrowding  821826   1.5    1.5    100
G25 Council Estates with Greatest Hardship  326507   0.6    0.6    100
H26 Multi-occupied Older Housing            200858   0.4    0.4    100
H27 Cosmopolitan Owner-occupied Terraces    572936   1.1    1.1    100
H28 Multi-let Housing in Cosmopolitan Areas 386503   0.7    0.7    100
H29 Better-off Cosmopolitan Areas           919979   1.7    1.7    100
I30 High Status Non-family Areas           1138397   2.1    2.1    100
I31 Multi-let Big Old Houses and Flats      834208   1.5    1.5    100
I32 Furnished Flats, Mostly Single People   296137   0.5    0.5    100
J33 Inter-war Semis, White Collar Workers  3072990   5.7    5.7    100
J34 Spacious Inter-war Semis, Big Gardens  2684265   5.0    5.0    100
J35 Villages with Wealthy Older Commuters  1582134   2.9    2.9    100
J36 Detached Houses, Exclusive Suburbs     1238441   2.3    2.3    100
K37 Private Houses, Well-off Older Residents 1218680   2.3    2.3    100
K38 Private Flats, Older Single People       845611   1.6    1.6    100
U39 Unclassified                            293884   0.5    0.5    100
        Area Total                        54086798  100.0  100.0

CACI Market Analysis          Source : 1981 CENSUS  ** CROWN COPYRIGHT **
01 404 0834              7-Dec-89                    ** CACI  COPYRIGHT **
© CACI Limited 1989
```

Figure 26 ACORN profile of Great Britain

The purpose of all the approaches to classification we have looked at is to simplify a complex world. The United Kingdom has over 56 million individual consumers, and no organisation can approach each one as an individual. Market research, by making use of consumer classifications, can help to group those 56 million people, and to subdivide them into manageable groups for whom products can be designed, and at whom promotion campaigns can be targeted.

Sampling the market

We started this chapter on commissioned market research by comparing modern organisations with the small craft business of the pre-industrial system. Because of the problems of communicating with today's large mass market, we have seen how advertising, complex distribution systems and, of course, market research have developed.

But market researchers cannot talk to all the members of a market unless that market is very small and concentrated. To talk to the whole market would be enormously expensive and time-consuming. For this reason surveys rely on smaller groups, or *samples*, which are selected to be *representative* of the *whole population*.

In this section we will look at the basic principles governing sampling and how samples are selected. You will meet a few useful statistical concepts and terms, but you won't be asked to do any calculations!

ACTIVITY

61

We have said that sampling is used because researching all the population wouldn't be feasible, but there is one exception to this 'rule'. Do you know what it is?

1 min

The Government, through its Office of Population, Census and Surveys (OPCS), carries out a count of the whole population every ten years; at the time of writing the next one is due in 1991. This decennial survey is the basis of a lot of the information we use in marketing, about the age, sex, social class and geographical profile of the United Kingdom.

However, even the OPCS, in order to obtain a fuller picture, undertakes a more detailed survey of a 10 per cent sample (that is, one in ten of the population).

How can we define a sample? Really any small part of something could be thought of as a sample. You might take a piece of curtain material as a sample to check against wallpaper, for example. In market research we are mainly concerned with a particular type of sample, a *random* sample of the population. This means that every member of the population has had an equal chance of being chosen for the research.

The term *population* doesn't just mean the population of the United Kingdom. A population can be any precisely defined group of people. It could be the population of Wales, or all the women over 16 in England, or every 16–19 year old in Scotland, or all firms employing less than 100 people in Northern Ireland. You can see that this definition includes not just people (it can include businesses, for example) and it can be defined by any characteristic. Some market researchers talk about the 'universe' rather than 'population', but it means the same thing.

ACTIVITY

62

10 mins

You work for a Local Authority as a Tourism Officer and you are interested in the views of visitors to your area on the holiday facilities available. List three factors you would use to define the population from which a sample could be drawn for a survey.

Compare your answers with the ones on page 135.

As we have noted, a random sample of a population means that in choosing some members to represent all of them, each member of the population should have an equal chance of being selected. This is harder than it seems; for a start it means that you need a list of all the members of a population from which to draw the sample. This is known as the *sampling frame*.

The only list of the *whole* population available at any time is the Census, and it is immediately out of date due to births and deaths! In any case, data on individual respondents is confidential so such a list is not available for use anyway.

Other lists are more selective. If the population which is of interest consists of members of a club or society, then the membership list is an ideal sampling frame. If the population is model train enthusiasts, then members of model train clubs or subscribers to specialist magazines provide an approximation to the population, but not all enthusiasts will be club members or journal subscribers. The sampling frame is sometimes called the 'working population', as it's the one we're working with rather than the actual population. So, we are faced with three problems in establishing our sampling frame:

● finding one which is up to date;
● finding one which is comprehensive;
● finding one which is accessible (i.e. not confidential).

The sampling frame which is most frequently used for general surveys of the adult population is the electoral register. This is updated every year, is in the public domain, and everyone over 18 is legally required to register (although not everybody does).

Having established a sampling frame, how do we choose a sample from it? Think back to the definition of a random sample; it's a sample of population where every member of the population has an equal chance of being selected.

ACTIVITY

63

5 mins

Look at the following samples. Which, if any, is being selected at random?

To choose a sample of the population in a town, researchers interviewed:
a) everybody living in two roads at either end of town;
b) every tenth household, working from street to street across the town;
c) every fifth person leaving the main car park in the town centre one Saturday.

Compare your answer with the one on page 136.

Systems to arrive at truly random samples can be quite expensive. Generally they involve allocating numbers to members of the population in the sampling frame and then selecting numbers mechanically (picking them out of a hat for example), electronically (using a random number generator program on a computer) or with published tables of random numbers.

Systems to arrive at truly random samples can be quite expensive

Unfortunately, if the population is spread over a large area a sample chosen by these methods could involve researchers in hours or days of travel simply to reach them. Of course, telephone surveys can solve this problem, although they, by definition, use a sampling frame which is based on telephone subscribers only.

An additional problem is that the physical process of numbering the population and then matching random numbers to them is immensely laborious, although modern computer systems can help overcome this. To solve these problems there are a variety of techniques which can be used to produce a sample which approximates to a truly random sample, but which eliminate some or all of the expenses and complexity.

One final point though, before we look at these; how big should a sample be? Obviously the larger the sample, the more accurately the sample reflects the population. (When the sample includes 100 per cent of the population it *is* the population!)

ACTIVITY

64

*

15 mins

This exercise is a good illustration of the principle of sampling. It takes a little time to prepare and is a bit fiddly! However you will find that it helps you to understand the key underlying principle of sampling.

To carry out the exercise you need a supply of dried beans (such as haricot beans) or something else of a similar size, and of uniform shape. Count out three piles, one of seventy beans, one of ten beans and one of twenty beans. Using different colour felt-tip pens mark each of the beans in the two smaller piles to identify them (e.g. ten blue and twenty red beans). Now you're ready to start – as long as the ink is dry – by putting all one hundred beans into a bowl and mixing them thoroughly. The bean mixture is your population.

Now shut your eyes and select ten beans, one at a time from the bowl. This is your first sample. Count how many you have chosen of the three types, blue, red and plain, write the figures down, put the beans back and repeat the experiment, selecting twenty beans this time. This is your second sample. Note the number of each type, put them back and repeat the experiment twice more with a sample of thirty and forty respectively. This gives you your third and fourth samples.

If your samples had exactly followed the make-up of the population, this experiment would have produced samples as follows:

Beans	Sample 1	Sample 2	Sample 3	Sample 4	Population
Plain	7	14	21	28	(70)
Blue	1	2	3	4	(10)
Red	2	4	6	8	(20)
Total	10	20	30	40	(100)

In fact it would be rare (though not impossible) to select samples exactly as described; what you probably found is that the sample proportions were closer to the population proportion as they got larger. The key question is how close do we want to get to exact population distributions, and how much do we want to pay? These two factors will determine the size of the sample to use, relative to the size of the population.

The final decision on sample size is best described as a trade-off; we have to trade-off precision for lower cost, or increase precision and accept higher costs. In practice, by accepting certain levels of accuracy (or 'significance') we can decide how big a sample to choose. The level of significance chosen is an indication of the degree of confidence or certainty we have that the results from our sample give a more-or-less accurate picture of the population from which the sample came. The two main levels of significance are the 95 per cent level (where we can have a nineteen out of twenty chance of knowing accurately about the population) or the 99 per cent level (where the chance of precision is ninety-nine out of a hundred).

Which level of significance (95 per cent or 99 per cent) do you think will be more expensive to achieve?

Compare your answer with the one on page 136.

Choosing a sample (the size having been decided on the basis of the degree of precision required) will normally be done in one of the following ways. Because of the difficulties involved in random sampling, none of them is truly random, but some do include a random process at some stage. On page 87 you will find Figure 28 which can be used to summarise the main features of each method. Fill in Figure 28 as you read through the description of each sampling method and then when you have filled in as much as you can, turn to page 88 where a completed version can be found for you to compare with yours.

Systematic samples select members of a population from a sampling frame by deciding what proportion of the population is needed for the sample (e.g. one in twenty involves selecting a sample of 50 from a population of 1000). A number between one and twenty is chosen by a random process as a starting point and then every twentieth person in the list thereafter is selected. If the starting point was 13, then number 13 and every twentieth person in the list thereafter (33, 53, 73 etc.) would be selected.

Although the systematic sample works well if different groups in the population are distributed randomly through the list, the danger exists of hitting a cycle. That is, if there is a regular pattern in the membership, this means one group could be missed, or only that group included. You met an example of this problem in Activity 63.

Stratified samples assume a basic knowledge of the characteristics of the population and are made up of a selection of samples from defined subparts (strata) of the population. For example, if we know the size of all the firms in an area listed in a trade directory (our sampling frame) we can select random samples from each size stratum (perhaps small firms, medium-sized firms, large firms). This ensures that all strata are represented in the sample. Of course we will need to define unambiguously what we mean by small, medium and large firms.

If the different strata are of varying sizes and contain different numbers of respondents we may draw different size samples proportionate to the size of the strata or equal size samples and weight the results to correct them to give the right proportion. For example, the Department of Employment's Labour Force Survey samples all large firms – of which there are few – but only 10 per cent of smaller firms.

Cluster samples are based on groupings (clusters) of the population in a given area. These can very often be based on local government or electoral districts, since the electoral registers can then be used as a sampling frame. Alternatively they can be all the residents of a block of flats or housing estate. The actual clusters used can be chosen at random and all the individuals in the cluster, or a random sample of them, then interviewed.

If the available clusters are of a different size or type it may be necessary to *stratify* them. This involves grouping the different clusters (e.g. District Council areas) by size or by urban/non-urban characteristics and then selecting a cluster from each group at random.

Multi-stage sampling involves combinations of levels of samples, often mixing the sampling methods (as with a stratified cluster sample). An example is shown in Figure 27. Multi-stage sampling enables the positive features of each system to be taken advantage of, in this case the sample chosen represents all the major strata in two wards from each of the six councils.

Stage	Characteristic	Sampling method
Stage 1	Group all District Councils into 'metropolitan' or 'shire' authorities.	Stratified
Stage 2	Subdivide both groups into 'large' or 'medium' or 'small' according to population.	Stratified
Stage 3	Select one authority at random from each of the six groups	Cluster
Stage 4	Select two electoral wards at random from each authority	Cluster
Stage 5	Select the sample from the electoral roll at intervals	Systematic

Figure 27 Multi-stage sampling using local authority areas

Purposive samples involve abandoning attempts to draw random (or quasi-random) samples. Instead they are set up by selecting members of the sample on purpose to reflect particular groups. For example, an exit sample from a shop might involve choosing all people (or a systematic sample such as every fourth person) leaving. A purposive sample defines a population according to some specific characteristic and then uses that characteristic as the basis for selection.

The reason it is a sample still, is that the members are used to provide information about a particular known population (e.g. all people in the catchment areas of the shop). For the purposive sample to be selected on purpose, the population it is drawn from and the basis on which the sample is being drawn must be identifiable.

Quota samples are really only a special kind of purposive sample; the sample is selected to match all the defined characteristics of the population. To do this it must be possible to divide the population accurately into groups in known proportions. A sample is then chosen to fit those characteristics in the right proportion.

An example of a quota sample would be one based on the population of women over fifteen grouped according to age and social class. Sixteen per cent of women are in social classes A and B combined (which is written as AB) and eleven per cent of women are in the age group 55–64. Therefore 1.8% (16% × 11%) of women will be 55–64 years old ABs. In a total

Quota samples are a specialist kind of purposive sample

sample of two thousand a quota of 36 (2000 × 1.8%) AB women aged 55–64 would be set.

An interviewer is instructed to seek out respondents to match the given quota; consequently there is no element of randomness in the sample unless the process is combined with another sampling method, say in a multi-stage system. For example, a number of parallel quota samples might be taken from a series of geographical areas selected at random.

ACTIVITY

66

→←

1 min

On page 70 we saw how questions to classify the respondents (for example, on age or social class) can be included in a number of positions in questionnaires. Whereabouts in the questionnaire do you think these would appear when a quota sample is used – at the beginning or the end?

As we have noted previously, in most sampling methods the classification questions tend to appear at the end, as they neatly round off an interview. Given the sensitivity some people have about their age or employment it is easier to ask questions about these issues once a relationship has been established. However, with a quota sample an interview is wasted if the respondent doesn't belong to the quota being sampled. For this reason a quota sample normally requires the classification question to be at the beginning of the questionnaire. 'Unwanted' respondents are then politely thanked and the interview ended.

We have looked briefly at a range of different methods of constructing a sample. Now we will go on to look at aspects of survey design, and show how the design of a survey helps to determine the sampling method.

	Systematic	Stratified	Cluster	Multi-stage	Purposive	Quota
Is there any truly random selection?						
Are all important sub-groups in population likely to be included?						
Is a sampling frame ('population list') needed?						
Can sample be confined to a limited geographical area?						
Are specific characteristics within the population needed to be known to construct the sample?						

Answers: Yes, Possibly, or No

Figure 28 Characteristics of sampling methods: complete the empty boxes as you learn about each sampling method

	Systematic	Stratified	Cluster	Multi-stage	Purposive	Quota
Is there any truly random selection?	Yes; to determine initial starting point	Yes; the selection from each stratum	Possibly; selection of geog. areas can be random	Yes; at any or all stages it is possible	No; sample selected due to identifiable characteristics	No; but well drawn quotes should match what a random sample would be
Are all important sub-groups in population likely to be included?	Possibly: if they have a regular (cyclic) appearance may be over or under represented	Yes; unless strata are defined so as to exclude them either intentionally or unintentionally	Possibly; if they are dispersed regularly in population, should be included	Possibly; depending on methods used	No; samples are drawn exclusively only from some sub-groups	Yes; a quota should be drawn deliberately to include all such groups, if known
Is a sampling frame ('population list') needed?	Yes; only possible if sampling frame available (can be a list of addresses)	Yes; some means needed to identify & separate different strata	Yes; some means needed to identify different clusters	Yes; as required by methods at each stage	No; sample can be selected by asking respondents to see if they fit requirements	No; sample can be selected by asking respondents to see if they fit requirements
Can sample be confined to a limited geographical area?	Possibly; depending on population and sampling frame used	Possibly; depending on population and sampling frame used	Yes; clusters are defined by geographical area!	Possibly; if a cluster sample is used, yes	Possibly; depending on population and characteristics being sampled	Possibly; depending on population and characteristics being sampled
Are specific characteristics within the population needed to be known to construct the sample?	No	Yes; strata are determined according to them	No	Possibly; depending on sampling methods used at different stages	Yes; particular characteristics needed to identify sample	Yes; particular characteristics needed to identify sample

Figure 29 Characteristics of sampling methods

Omnibus surveys

Omnibus surveys provide some useful examples of the ideas we have been looking at in this chapter. The name refers to their capacity to 'pick-up' questions, the answers to which will be of interest to various organisations, just as a bus picks up passengers from bus stops.

Omnibus surveys are not commissioned by a particular organisation but initiated by the MR agency itself, which identifies a particular target group of individuals to concentrate on.

Organisations which are likely to be interested in the results of the survey are offered the opportunity to purchase the analysis, and to include their own topics in the questionnaire. The Target Group Index, which we mentioned earlier, is an example of an omnibus survey. The identification of a particular target market which will interest particular organisations leads most omnibus surveys to use a quota sampling design. In Figure 30 you will see an example of this, the Harris Research Centre's *Young Person's Omnibus*.

ACTIVITY

67

5–10 mins

You work in the marketing department of a company manufacturing fashionable clothes for teenagers. The Young Person's Omnibus *could be a useful mechanism for researching the market. Write down a list of issues which you could ask Harris to include questions about in the survey.*

Compare your list with the one on page 136.

The advantage to an organisation of using an omnibus survey, as long as its target market is appropriate, is the relatively low cost compared with commissioning original research. As the *Young Person's Omnibus* shows, there are discounts available if only a limited part of the survey quota is of interest. This offers an opportunity to reduce costs further.

Of course, omnibus surveys have limitations. Because the survey has a predefined quota this can only be varied within set limits to meet the requirements of particular organisations. Also, the range and type of questions which can be included may be limited by the interview method or to avoid clashes with questions from other organisations. Commissioned original research is like a taxi, it takes you exactly where you want to go. Omnibus surveys follow predetermined routes; if they go close to where you want to go, use them. Otherwise take a taxi, if you can afford it!

Figure 30

YOUNG PERSONS OMNIBUS

THE FACTS ON TODAY'S YOUTH

If your product or service is aimed at young people, if you need to know more about the youth of today, we have the answer. It's simple, highly flexible yet extremely cost effective. **Young Persons Omnibus.**

A National Sample...

Young Persons Omnibus uses a nationally representative base sample of males and females between 12 and 24 years of age. The sample is structured by individual year of age e.g. 120 twelve year olds, 130 seventeen year olds, etc. This generates a total sample size of 1500 – split 770 males and 730 females. In addition to sex and age quotas, the sample is also controlled by social class (based upon head of household).

...And Nationwide Interviews

Interviewing is conducted at 100 standard sampling points to ensure national accuracy and comparability. So if you need a tracking survey, or 'pre- and post-' response, get it from Young Persons Omnibus.

As Flexible as Youth Itself

Young Persons Omnibus can be easily and quickly tailored to match your precise requirements. We can, for example, provide a minority sample – 16-24 year-olds, say, or 12-15 year-old males.

We can also boost your sample in a particular way – say by increasing the number of 12-14 year-olds from 355 to 500.

We can even extend the overall age range by adding older respondents – those between the ages of 25 and 34, for instance. By choosing the correct proportional mix, we can provide a balanced sample from 12 right through to 34 years.

Client Service

Whichever sample you choose, our executives are there to lend a hand with everything from initial advice on questionnaire design, through to analysis requirements. Our executives can also provide, when required, full interpretive reports at particularly competitive rates.

Young Persons Omnibus. It could hardly be simpler. Or more comprehensive.

To book your survey, or for further information, call Mike Watson on 01-948 5011.

And ask for **Young Persons Omnibus.**

FEES AND DISCOUNTS

Our standard rate card lists fees based on 1500 respondents. There are, however, a number of significant extra discounts –

Reduced Sample Discount

We can provide a discount for work involving only part of the total sample e.g. Males only, 12-16 year olds. Depending on the sample size, the following discounts apply to our full rates:

Sample Size	Discount
Up to 500	50%
750	40%
1000	20%
1250	8%
1500	nil

(Sample Size discount does not apply to Entry Fee or Showcards.)

Continuous Links/Regular Subscriber Discounts

Discounts are also available when two or more links are commissioned using the same sample and questionnaire (a 'pre- and post-' survey, for example).

TIMINGS

The Young Persons Omnibus is operated quarterly in February, May, August and November. Tabulations follow fieldwork approximately four weeks after the last date for questions. For precise timings and deadlines, call Mike Watson on 01-948 5011.

The Harris Research Centre

Holbrooke House Holbrooke Place
34-38 Hill Rise Richmond Surrey TW10 6UA
Telephone 01-948 5011. Telex 24403 LHIIUKG
Fax 01-948 6335.

Research analysis and application

So far in this chapter we have looked at:

● the commissioning of market research;
● question and questionnaire design;
● consumer classification;
● sampling principles and methods; and
● omnibus surveys.

Ultimately, the value of market research depends on the analysis of survey data and using what has been discovered in a constructive way. As we have already seen, market research can't make decisions for you, but it can provide you with more information on which you can base decisions.

In this final section of Chapter 3 we will look at some of the techniques used to analyse the results of a market research survey, and the ways in which those results can be used.

ACTIVITY

68

10 mins

Figure 31 below is an extract from the report by Donald Osborne Research Ltd of the research carried out for ABTA. It presents a detailed analysis of the response to Question 13, 'What sort of accommodation was provided?'. Look at this set of figures and see what conclusions you can draw from them about the relationship between holidaymakers' age and the type of accommodation they choose.

DESCRIPTION OF ACCOMMODATION PROVIDED

Q.13a "What sort of accommodation was provided?"

	ANALYSED BY AGE						
	TOTAL	15–24	25–34	35–44	45–54	55–64	65+
BASE:							
(ALL WHO READ BROCHURES)	700	80	116	171	111	130	92
	%	%	%	%	%	%	%
TYPE OF ACCOMMODATION:							
HOTEL/PENSION ETC	66	56	51	53	78	77	83
VILLA (SELF-CATERING)	18	21	28	23	12	11	9
APARTMENT/FLAT	9	13	14	11	6	9	3
CHALET/CABIN/CARAVAN	4	7	4	9	1	2	3
TENTS	2	3	2	4	1	–	–
OTHERS	1	–	–	–	2	1	3

Figure 31 Extract from ABTA survey

Compare your answers with the ones on page 136.

This table is a typical example of *cross tabulation*; the table of data has been constructed by analysing answers to one question (Question 13a) on the basis of answers to another question (Age classification). More complex cross tabulations can combine responses to more than one question across one or both arms of the table (e.g. sub-dividing age groups into males and females). An example of this is shown below in Figure 32, a further extract from the ABTA survey.

HEALTH INSURANCE

Q.22a "Did you have any health insurance on holiday?"
Q.22b "Where did you get your insurance?"

ANALYSED BY AGE

	ALL RESPONDENTS	15–34	35–54	55+
BASE:(INTERVIEWS)	%	%	%	%
WITH TRAVEL INSURANCE	95	92	95	96
BOUGHT FROM:				
TRAVEL AGENT/TOUR OP.	87	85	86	89
OWN INSURANCE COMPANY	3	3	4	2
INSURANCE BROKER	2	–	2	3
OTHERS	2	2	2	1
DON'T KNOW	1	2	1	1

Figure 32

Source: 'Holiday Satisfaction Survey': Donald Osborne Research Ltd. for the Association of British Travel Agents.

Clearly, only those respondents having health insurance could go on to answer Q. 22b 'Where did you get your insurance?' This is an example of 'routeing', which we looked at earlier.

More complex forms of analysis which can be used involve a range of statistical techniques. It is beyond the scope of this Workbook to look at these in great detail. However it is useful to know what they can do, and so they are briefly introduced here:

Significance testing is related to the ways of determining sample size we encountered earlier. A test of significance can tell you whether a difference in results from different groups (like the age and accommodation cross tabulation in Figure 32) is likely to be a real difference, or if it is something which has occurred by chance.

Correlation measures the strength of the relationship between two sets of statistics; for example, height and weight are *positively correlated;* as one goes up, so does the other. *Negative correlation* means things go in opposite direction; for example, electricity consumption goes up as the air temperature goes down.

Positive correlation   Negative correlation

It is very important when using correlation techniques to be wary of the difference between correlation and causation; just because the two things change in line with each other doesn't necessarily mean one causes the other.

ACTIVITY
69

The figures below (Figure 33) are from the Department of Employment's Census of Employment, 1981. They show the number of census units (work places) for each size band of the number of employees in the workplace. Does the number of work places appear correlated to their size; if so is it positive or negative correlation?

5 mins

Size bands according to numbers of employees	Census units numbers
1	114,163
2	128,901
3–4	184,884
5–10	257,890
11–24	163,997
25–49	69,620
50–99	33,463
100–199	17,684
200–499	9,866
500–999	2,789
1,000–1,999	1,166
2,000–4,999	417
5,000+	64
Total	984,904

*All of these figures exclude Order 1 of the Standard Industrial Classification (agriculture, forestry and fishing) 1968.

Source: Department of Employment, Statistics Division, 1985.

Figure 33

Compare your answer with the one on page 136.

Factor analysis is a rather complicated statistical technique which is used to identify the effect of various factors in determining behaviour. Most lifestyle classifications have been devised by using factor analysis to identify the strength of various characteristics, or factors, in determining behaviour. By looking for clusters of factors it is possible to identify the people exhibiting that cluster as belonging to a discrete group. If you look back at the SAGACITY lifestyles on page 78 you will see how such clusters of factors identify groups, in this case age and dependents, income and occupation.

ACTIVITY

70

10 mins

You are the Marketing Manager for an importer of low-priced East European cars. You are considering introducing four-wheel drive options on mid-range models.

Market research using factor analysis has identified that there are four distinct groups who buy four-wheel drive versions of saloon and hatchback cars:

a) *Professional people of all ages, such as vets and agricultural engineers, in rural areas;*

b) *Sales representatives and others, aged 25–44, who do a lot of 'company' driving including a substantial proportion outside urban areas:*

c) *C1 and C2 families aged 30–44, with children aged 5–16, who own and tow caravans for holidays;*

d) *AB singles and young couples under 30, living in urban areas, and with above average incomes.*

Which of these groups would you think most appropriate to target and why?

Compare your answer with the one on page 136.

As this example shows, having used the techniques for data collection and analysis which are most appropriate, we then have to decide what the research is telling us, and how it can affect our decision-making. Once again we come back to the marketing mix; marketing research enables us to consider the different elements of the mix, singly or together, and decide whether any changes are needed to any of them.

It is possible to identify a whole range of changes to the Product which might result from market research, and in Chapter 4 we will look at them in more detail. These include design changes to the product (including its packaging); the introduction of new and complementary products, or variations on the existing one; a move into new product areas; or a decision to delete products from the product range.

All such Product changes could arise from researching the market and identifying patterns of demand and attitudes to (potential) products. Equally it's possible to find out how the market reacts (or would react) to variations in Promotional strategies or Pricing.

The ABTA survey we have looked at several times in this chapter was concerned primarily with distributors (since travel agents are primarily retail outlets for tour operators) and thus with Place. The primary objective of the survey was to assess the degree of holiday satisfaction felt by consumers. It was able to detect the differences in satisfaction with the Product which were beyond travel agents' control, and those which were attributable to the agents themselves at the point of purchase.

One further result of this particular piece of research provides an interesting example of the use of such surveys. ABTA obtained extensive coverage of the survey results in the national press; this publicity would have cost substantially more than the £10,000 cost of the survey, if it had all been 'paid for' advertising.

Furthermore, media coverage of the ABTA survey came just before the release by *Holiday Which?* of its annual survey of the holiday experiences of Consumers' Association members. Since the CA had frequently been critical in the past, this well-timed publicity most effectively defused any negative comments they might have made.

In Chapter 3 we have covered a large number of issues and techniques connected with market research; their importance lies very much in how they can be used to obtain information which can make marketing more effective. In Chapter 4, on product development, you will find a number of examples of the use of market information in shaping product decisions.

The following Activity brings together the general concepts we have covered in this chapter.

ACTIVITY

71

30–40 mins

You are a recently appointed Assistant Brand Manager for an fmcg company. The Marketing Manager has just given you an extract from a report by a market researcher about the product which you are involved in marketing. You are asked to rewrite this data for a short item to appear in the company's internal newsletter, which is distributed to 2500 employees from the factory floor to the Board of Directors. You are restricted to about 100 words.

Market researcher's report
'We initially conducted some qualitative research with 4 groups of 8 women, all in the age range 25–44. Three groups were predominantly C1/C2, and one AB. On the basis of unstructured group discussions it became clear that unprompted recall of the company's brands was low, compared with companies X and Y. Similarly the image of the brand was rather old-fashioned, reliable but not very exciting.

'To test these findings, a survey was made of 2000 households, using a multi-stage sample; eight electoral wards were selected, four each in the South East and North West, two urban and one each suburban and rural in each region. Women in 250 households in each ward were interviewed, in a quota based on age and social class. Unprompted recall of the company's brand name was only 23% compared to 71% and 68% for companies X and Y respectively. Analyses by age and social class showed no significant differences on recall for companies X and Y (at the 95% level) but the company's brand name was recalled primarily by older women (45+) in social classes C2D (again, significant at the 95% level).

When asked to rate the three brands on a semantic differential scale reliable/unreliable, amongst those having prompted or unprompted recall of each brand, the company's brand scored higher than its competitors, an average of 2.1 'reliable', against 1.8 for company X and 0.9 for company Y.'

How does your news item compare with the one we have written on page 137?

Now work through the Second Progress Test below. When you are happy with your progress, move on to Chapter 4.

SECOND PROGRESS TEST

Try to answer each question without referring to the text. When you have answered all the questions you can, you should look up the correct answers on page 141.

1   Market research supplies information from _____

    to _____ .

2   The two main professional bodies for market researchers are

    a)

    b)

3   The eight most commonly used market research survey designs are:

    a)   e)

    b)   f)

    c)   g)

    d)   h)

4   Which of the research designs you listed above is most likely to need to use prizes or other incentives to encourage people to participate?

5   Questions tend to be of two types, _____

    or _____ .

6   What could you use to encourage people to recognise particular answers when conducting a survey?

7   What is meant by a 'probe' when administering a question or interview?

8　In what sort of scaling method would each of the following questions be used?

　　a) List the following statements in your order of preference.

　　b) Look at the following statements; for each say if you strongly agree/agree/uncertain/disagree/strongly disagree.

9　Items are listed in order to produce this type of scale: stratified; orderly; interval; ordinal; absolute. Underline the correct term.

10 a) What is wrong with this proposed questionnaire item?

　　　You do agree that embryo research is a bad thing   YES/NO

　　b) What effect would it have on the results of the survey?

11　What is the principal determinant of social class in both the JICNARS and Registrar-General's grading systems?

12　Here are the six JICNARS Social Grades. Write the correct social status alongside each one.

　　A

　　B

　　C1

　　C2

　　D

　　E

13　Which of these grades would

　　a) a skilled craftsman, and
　　b) an old age pensioner on state pension, belong to?

14　What term is used to describe classification systems based on where people live?

15　What market research concept are 'Yuppies' an example of?

16　What statistically is the most valid sample? Underline the correct response:

　　random; large;, stratified; duplicated; biased.

17　A list of a population from whom a sample is drawn is called a

18 Which level of significance gives more reliable and exact results, 95% or 99%?

19 A sample is drawn so that every fifth member of a population is included. This is called a random

organised
cluster } sample.
systematic
interval

Underline the correct response.

20 A sample drawn from all known groups within a population is called a strategic

cluster
random } sample.
opportunity
stratified

Underline the correct response.

21 A sample drawn from a geographically limited area is called a(n) neighbourhood

electoral } sample.
cluster
map

Underline the correct response.

22 A quota sample is a particular kind of _____
sample.

23 What name is given to a survey that allows organisations to use market research without commissioning their own surveys?

24 If two sets of figures move up or down together they are said to be

25 When answers to one question in a survey are analysed on the basis of answers to another question, the result is described as a

Now check your answers on page 141.

4 Product Development

After working through this chapter you will be aware of how new products are developed and launched, and be able to use various techniques for identifying new market opportunities and for analysing strengths and weaknesses in a product range. You will also be able to explain the use of test markets, and identify the features of a market which make it suitable for testing new products.

Introduction

Where do new products come from? Are they the result of extensive market research to identify customer needs, or do they stem from innovative research in laboratories, workshops and design studios?

Where do new products come from?

In this chapter we will look first of all at the question 'What is a product?' We will then go on to consider how market opportunities are identified, and at the way new products are developed and the lives of old ones extended. We will also be looking at how new products are tested in the market and how individual products fit into a *portfolio* of products, that is the whole range of products provided by an organisation.

Curiously enough in a chapter on product development we shall also consider divestment, the reduction in the product portfolio through the ending of the supply of products. For it's not only brand new products we're looking at, but the development of products throughout their life.

Think of a product – a good or service – which you purchase regularly. How has that product been developed (if at all) during the period in which you have been a customer? See if you can identify what those changes were designed to achieve. Write down your observations – we will return to them later.

What is 'the product'?

You already know that the word 'product' can be used to describe goods and services, but before we look at the process of product development we need to be clear about what 'the product' actually consists of.

To start with we will concentrate on goods, as they are easier to describe and visualise. However, we will also be looking at services to see how the same principles can be applied to them.

The product 'onion'

Figure 34 illustrates what is known as the 'onion' concept. At its centre is the physical entity (the core product); around this are the layers which marketing adds to the product. These accumulate until at the outer rim is the insubstantial but very real brand image developed for this product. This 'augmented' product is the total of all these layers, and is the product being marketed.

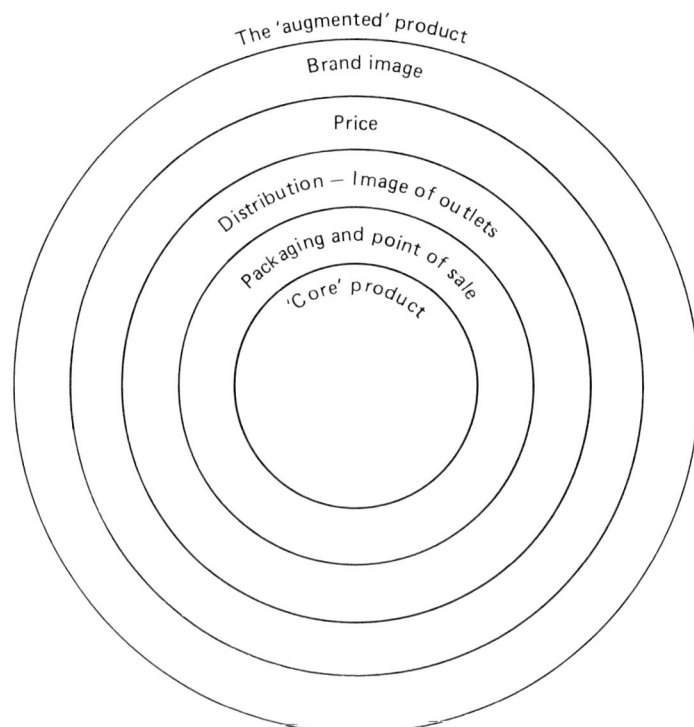

Figure 34 The product 'onion'

Go back to the example you thought of for the last Activity; were the changes you noted changes in the physical product, or were they changes in one of the outer layers of the onion?

Looking at the product in this way shows that it can be changed in many ways without actually changing the goods or services which lie at the heart of the product onion.

The best way to understand how the 'onion' is built up is to consider a simple example which illustrates the build up from a core product to a final augmented product.

The core product

Having identified a core product – let us use an ordinary sandwich – we then have to recognise that it can come in more than one variety. Variations are possible in the bread (white, brown, malted, etc.), in the spread (butter, polyunsaturated fat, ordinary margarine, etc.), in the filling, and in the shape (sliced bread, fingers, rolls etc.).

Decisions about dealing with such variations are fundamental to our marketing strategy. Is this a low cost, high volume market, or a high cost 'niche' market? Or are we aiming for something in between? Clearly we need to look at the marketing opportunities and our resource capabilities; later in this chapter we will be looking at identifying market opportunities in some detail, but we must also be aware of what any organisation is actually able to do.

Draw up a list of all the outlets you know in your locality which sell sandwiches. What sort of resources do they have? (In other words, do they rely on large kitchens, staff, etc., are they small and specialist, or do they buy in products?) Write down your list – we will use it again later.

As we already know, an organisation needs to match what it can do to the markets available. If there is no market for its particular type of output, or an inadequate market, it is the organisation that must change, not the market. (In the fourth Workbook in this series we will look at the wider implications of this in 'Marketing Planning'.)

Packaging

Having decided on the product we now need to look at packaging. Does the product need any packaging? Packaging can serve a number of functions, so our decision about packaging must consider all of these factors.

ACTIVITY

75

5 mins

Why do products have to be packaged? Draw up a list of functions which packaging of various types can perform, then read on.

Packaging exists primarily to protect a product, in storage and in transit. The more delicate a product is, and the rougher the handling to which it will be subjected, the more care needs to be devoted to packaging.

Packaging can also help in handling; products which are awkward to carry, or to stack, can be packaged to make them easier to handle. Packaging can also convert bulk goods into standard units – bags of sugar or flour, boxes of washing powder or tea. This process is often referred to as unitisation.

Packaging can have a point-of-sale purpose as well; on the retail shelf it can serve as a promotional vehicle (the 'silent salesman'). This is accomplished by its design and the way it presents the product, and by the use of selling messages and promotional devices. In some cases the packaging can serve as a promotional device in its own right, for example by selling coffee in containers which are re-usable as storage jars.

One important element in the packaging decision is how the product is going to be distributed; clearly the level of protection, the ease of handling and the importance of unitisation and any promotional purpose are determined by how distribution takes place.

In the case of our sandwiches, no individual packaging may be needed if we are selling them to eat in a cafe or restaurant, although mass storage and hygiene require some sort of protection to be provided. If they are sold to be taken away, then some form of wrapper will be required (a paper bag?); if they are made centrally and distributed to outlets then individual containers such as the clear, stiff plastic cartons used in many retail stores are needed.

Of course, packaging may not always serve a positive purpose. Some people argue that money is wasted on over-packaging goods, leading to environmental disadvantages. Anyone who has had to fight their way into a 'bubble' pack to get out new batteries, or who has waded through city centre litter, may well have strong opinions on the subject!

Packaging and image

Let's consider the different image of two contrasting types of sandwich packaging, a paper bag and a clear plastic container. Image is the mental idea or picture which is conjured up by something; the clear plastic carton might, for example, suggest 'hygiene' to you.

ACTIVITY

76

What other 'images' are suggested by a paper bag on the one hand and a clear plastic container on the other? Write a short list of words or phrases which each suggests.

3 mins

Compare your list with the one on page 137.

The choice between a paper bag, a plastic carton, a plain cardboard box, or a four-colour printed carton says something about the product; the packaging changes the nature of the product the customer buys. As a product is designed questions about the intended image and likely packaging have to be taken into account.

Packaging services

Service industries often talk about packaging to describe the way particular services are designed and presented to the public. Although they have no physical packaging, the same effect can be achieved. Putting together a particular mix of services and offering them as a 'job lot' has the same effect as unitised packaging in making 'handling' (processing the service) easier. It can be promoted by pre-prepared materials bundled together. And the service is protected from 'damage in transit' by employees, brokers or agents who may damage it by misrepresenting or badly describing it. Figure 35 illustrates this by showing one of the current accounts offered by the Midland Bank, which is 'packaged' to bring together a group of services targeted at a particular market.

Distribution

As we have seen, the distribution system selected for a product will determine the type of packaging needed. But it also says something about the product being bought. Stores, catalogues, mail order, telephone sales, door-to-door selling, agents and brokers, all have their own images. The products they sell are themselves shaped by those images.

ACTIVITY

77

Look back at the list of outlets you drew up in answer to Activity 74. What adjectives spring to mind to describe the image each of those outlets has for you?

10 mins

- CardWise — a comprehensive card protection scheme.

- Personal Legal Assistance. providing:-
  — 24 hour telephone legal advisory service
  — legal expenses insurance up to £10.000. per claim.

- Midland eurocheque card and eurocheques.

Full details. including terms and conditions and any exclusions where applicable of the services included in Orchard Option appear in your customer guide.

ORCHARD OPTION

A special package of services offering even greater financial flexibility and security for just £5 a month.

- £100 AutoCheque Card — to guarantee your cheques up to £100. twice the limit of most cards. You can also use your card to transfer funds between your Orchard Account and Orchard Savings. at Midland cash machines. And. you can still use your card at any Switch outlet.

- Motor Assistance — a comprehensive breakdown recovery service.

- Purchase Safeguard — automatic insurance for your Midland Access and Midland Visa purchases.

- Personal Accident Cover — up to £20.000 cash in the event of accidental death or total and permanent disablement.

Reproduced by permission of Midland Bank plc

Figure 35 Packaging a service

The control an organisation has over the distribution system and outlets for its products varies a good deal. Some have their own outlets; others restrict sales to particular, specialist, outlets; some allow their products to be sold freely wherever they can.

Pricing

Once again there is an interrelationship between the layers of the product 'onion' already described and the pricing strategy adopted. Pricing says a lot about a product, as well as how much it costs!

For example, with no other information about a ham sandwich than that it costs 32p, or £1.19, your expectations about the product will be quite different. You wouldn't expect to pay 32p in Marks and Spencer, or in the tea-rooms at the Ritz; you would regard £1.19 as over-priced at a mobile snack bar on a lay-by off the A1!

Research has shown that people's perceptions of price and price ranges affect their perceptions of the product. Little differences like 99p rather than £1, or £1.59 rather than £1.60 can be important, even though there are often complaints from consumers about such pricing strategies.

If you are going to buy something you will have some expectation of how much you want to pay. Usually that will be a price range rather than a fixed figure. You will have a top price, above which it will be too expensive, and a bottom price below which you may feel it's too cheap, and the quality must have suffered.

ACTIVITY

78

2–3 mins

Look at the following list of products. What would you consider to be the sort of price range you would expect to pay (not like to be able to pay) if you were to buy the product? Jot down your answers next to each one.

- *A new (or second-hand) car*
- *A foreign holiday (per person)*
- *An evening meal out (per person)*
- *A new suit or dress*
- *A take-away sandwich!*

If possible, get a friend to complete the same Activity without looking at your price ranges. Are there any differences?

There's no right or wrong answer to this Activity. Each person has their own expectations. In the next Workbook we will be looking at pricing strategies in far more detail, and you will get a chance to see the effect pricing can have on consumers' perceptions of products and purchase decisions.

Brand image

Let's get back to the example of our sandwich. The development of the product has progressed from its physical characteristics, through its packaging and distribution, to deciding on pricing. The final level is to decide what brand image we are going to have for the product. Branding and brand strategies determine the overall marketing concept of the product as it is presented to the customer. This means the perception the customer will have of the product – its quality and status, the way it will enhance their life – as well as just its physical characteristics.

Later in this chapter we will look at branding in more detail; however we can finish this section by introducing the idea and asking this question:

'What image do we want customers to have of the product?'

Is it;

- a snack;
- a light meal;
- a convenience food;
- a chance to experiment with new fillings;
- a traditional food;
- a common-or-garden activity;
- part of a special treat?

From a mobile snack bar to a take-away sandwich bar, a British Rail buffet car, a high street retailer, a country pub, or five-star luxury hotel, the same basic product can be presented in a multitude of ways. These are the effects of marketing in developing the product.

ACTIVITY

79

5 mins

Consider the product you selected for Activity 72 again. How is it marketed? What image do you have of the product (if any), other than as something which fulfils its basic function? Choose some adjectives which describe your perceptions of the product.

●●●

CASE STUDY: Roys of Wroxham

The image generated by a company can change as the core product and the market changes. Roys describes itself as 'the world's largest village store' and its premises dominate the centre of Wroxham, the Norfolk village in which it is based.

The 'village store' consists of a 13,000-square-foot supermarket, 35,000-square-foot department store, plus a DIY store, a garden centre and a fashion shop 'Miss Roy'. Over the years, however, the range of outlets has changed, and the image the store projects has changed with it.

During the 1970s the store emphasised low prices, and developed its promotional strategies to reinforce this – the message was snappy, direct and uncompromisingly pushed their low prices above all else. Today the

market has changed; low prices are still there, but tied to high quality and with emphasis on the opportunity to enjoy a visit to Roys as a benefit in its own right.

The product on offer at Roys is now a leisure experience rather than a shopping trip. It includes the opportunity to combine browsing through the shops, taking a boat out on the Broads (Wroxham is the major centre for boating holidays) and enjoying the countryside. These are all part of 'the product'.

The image has also changed, with a new logo and completely refurbished outlets in neutral colours rather than the brasher displays of earlier years. Underlying these changes has been an awareness of the market and constant monitoring of market information to ensure the company responds quickly to any changes.

●●●

Identifying new market opportunities

For a market-centred organisation like Roy's, the key to product development is the identification of new market opportunities. These are opportunities to sell:

- new products to existing customers (new product development);
- existing products to new customers (market development);
- new products to new customers (diversification).

ACTIVITY

80

>←

3–5 mins

Figure 36 shows an example of what is known as an Ansoff Matrix, named after its originator Igor Ansoff. The top left box is the current position (existing products in existing markets). Which boxes do 'new product development', 'market development' and 'diversification' fit into?

	Existing products	New products
Existing markets	Current position	_____ _____
New markets	_____ _____	_____ _____

Figure 36 The Ansoff Matrix

Compare your answers with the completed matrix on page 137.

In all three developmental strategies, whether increasing the products sold to existing customers, or developing new customers, the organisation needs to identify the opportunities in the market place. To do this it relies on its market information systems.

Remind yourself what MIS consists of by looking back to Figure 1 on page 18.

Market information

The information coming in from the market, from the sales force, desk research and commissioned market research can all serve to identify new market opportunities. But can the market identify new products which don't actually exist yet? If you think about it, can you imagine products which you would like to have but have not been invented or developed? You might be able to think of what a product can do but is that the same as thinking of the product itself?

In fact information from the market is more likely to identify types of new market opportunity:

- opportunities for existing products in new market areas;
- opportunities to copy other successful products in new or existing markets (sometimes called a 'me too' strategy);
- opportunities to satisfy customer needs (for example, more convenience in preparing hot snacks or more safety in cars).

ACTIVITY

81

➤❮

2 mins

Look at the three opportunities above; which strategies in the Ansoff Matrix do they help? Don't read on until you have answered this.

The first one helps the market development strategy, the other two both help the product development and diversification strategies. However, you can imagine that 'me too-ism' (copying another organisation's product) is easier than having to develop a completely new product to satisfy needs which have been identified and which existing products don't satisfy.

It is generally recognised that innovation, designing and producing completely new products has severe drawbacks.

ACTIVITY

82

🖉

3 mins

What specific drawbacks can you think of to be considered by a company which might wish to become involved in product innovation?

Write down your answer and compare it with the one on page 138.

These drawbacks really fall into two areas, those connected with perfecting the product, and those connected with developing the market.

The drawbacks to innovation

If a completely new product is being launched it is prone to technical hitches – the problems associated with untried and untested products. Many people are reluctant to buy radically new models of cars during their first year to avoid these sorts of problems.

Innovation also raises the question of whether the product does actually satisfy market demand. In the next section we will look at the techniques to help in finding out the answer to this question.

A completely new product may be prone to technical hitches

The problems of establishing a new market are primarily financial; it can be very expensive to convince customers that they do want a product which they have done without for so long! It is for this reason that many firms are very happy to be second into the market. Once another firm has spent the necessary money on establishing a market (which in consumer markets may run into millions), they can come in fresh and start to exploit this new market created by their competitors.

ACTIVITY

83

1 min

Can you think of any recent examples of companies choosing to come second into the market? Sometimes it's not that obvious because the 'me too' company will often try to mimic the product of the original innovator to take advantage of all the promotion! Make a note of any examples you can think of.

Compare your ideas with our suggestions on page 138.

Finding new market opportunities is one thing; being able to exploit them successfully is quite different – in the fmcg industry ('fast moving consumer goods'), for example, it is generally accepted that only 25 per cent of new product launches will succeed!

So far we have looked at the four choices in product development open to an organisation (the Ansoff Matrix):

- stay in the same market with the same product(s);
- develop new products;
- develop new markets for existing products;
- diversify into new markets with new products.

We have also seen that MIS can help by identifying opportunities (although not by designing new products!). And finally we have seen some of the difficulties of innovation associated with the development of completely new products to satisfy identified needs.

In the next section we will work our way through the product development process, seeing how MIS can be employed in a practical way, and how products can be tested to minimise the difficulties of innovation.

Developing a new product

In practice new product ideas rarely come in a flash of inspiration; they tend to emerge over time as a result of:

- original research by designers, engineers, scientists, etc; leading to opportunities for innovative products;
- development of existing products to the point that a complete redesign becomes inevitable;
- shifts in demand for existing products, pointing to the need for innovative or redesigned products;
- identification of opportunities to exploit markets by copying other companies' products ('me-too');
- speculative market research identifying market gaps which existing products do not fill.

●●

CASE STUDY: *The Independent*

The market for national daily papers in the United Kingdom can be divided into three main segments:

- 'mass market' tabloids (*Sun, Daily Mirror, Daily Star*);
- 'middle market' tabloids (*Daily Mail, Daily Express, Today*);
- 'quality' broadsheets (*The Times, Guardian, Daily Telegraph*).

It was in this latter segment that the founders of *The Independent* believed that there was a market opportunity. Their reasoning was based on a number of features of the peculiar market for newspapers:

- the political complexion of the existing broadsheets;
- the closure of *The Times* for nearly a year, due to industrial problems;
- the recent acquisition of *The Times* by News International Group, which was felt by some readers to compromise its traditional image;
- the decline of sales in the middle market, suggesting there might be some readers willing to 'trade up'.

It was this analysis of the existing market which led Andreas Whittam Smith to propose the establishment of the new paper.

●●

ACTIVITY

84

➔←

2 mins

Which of the five categories of product development do you think the introduction of The Independent *fits into?*

The Independent wasn't a totally innovative newspaper (as *Today* claimed to be), nor was it a redesign of an existing product (which was how the *Sun* emerged). To some extent *The Independent* was similar to other 'quality' papers, but it set out deliberately to establish itself as being different (and 'independent').

Existing papers appeared to be failing to fulfil existing demand either because the demand had changed, or, as some readers believed the papers themselves had changed.

Whittam Smith's belief, backed up by market research, was that a segment of the market wanted a quality paper which did not have an overt political line. It was very much this perception of a market gap (the last category on our list) which led to *The Independent*'s launch.

In contrast, the launch of the Sinclair C5 electric vehicle, very much based in category 1, shows how a technology-led product development policy has its pitfalls! There is an important distinction between being able to produce a product and there being a market demand for that product.

That is the essential difference between product-centred and market-centred approaches to innovation.

Original research and product development

A market-centred approach to new product development does not necessarily exclude original research. There is a difference however between 'pure' research and 'market-led' research. Look at the diagram in Figure 37; you will see that much research and development leading to new product development does rely on 'pure' research.

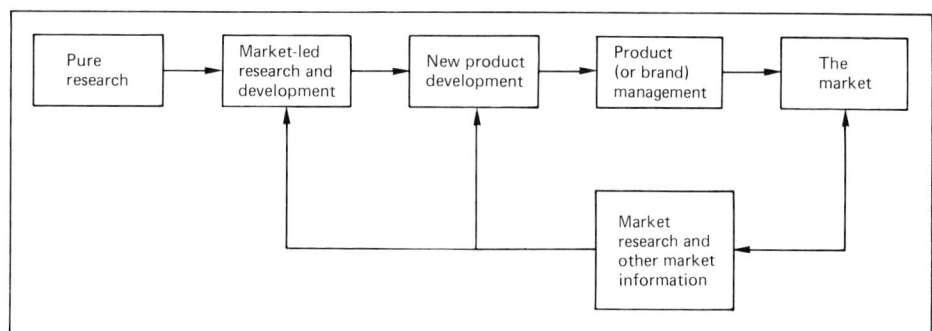

Figure 37 'Pure' research and product development

Such research can take place in colleges, universities and in private reearch institutes. It's not just scientific research either; social policy research can influence the shape of new public service 'products' (health care, education, social services etc.) The point at which such original ideas start being converted into marketable products, using information about the market, represents a point at which a change in the nature of the research is required.

ACTIVITY

85

5–10 mins

Research laboratories have isolated a compound which, when inhaled as a vapour, is an effective analgesic (painkiller) with no apparent side-effects. As Product Manager in a drugs company, you are considering market research to identify whether the product is worth pursuing. Remembering the processes involved in devising questions for MR to answer (described in the last chapter), what questions would you want answered?

Compare your answers with the ones on page 138.

Clearly the development of a marketable product would depend on consumer reaction to the potential 'primary' product, and the way it is presented. Thus the pure research leads into market-led research and development, and ultimately the development of a new product.

From original research to the market

As we have seen, the ideas encouraging research and development can come from the market as well as from pure research. They may come from a need to find new ways of presenting existing products to meet changes in the market, or to copy other organisation's products, or to fill an identified gap.

The point at which research and development becomes new product development is a critical one. The diagram in Figure 38 expands on Figure 37 to emphasise the roles played at different stages. This doesn't mean that different people fulfil these roles. In the smallest organisations they may be all the same person! In large multinationals, there may be separate companies responsible for some of the different elements.

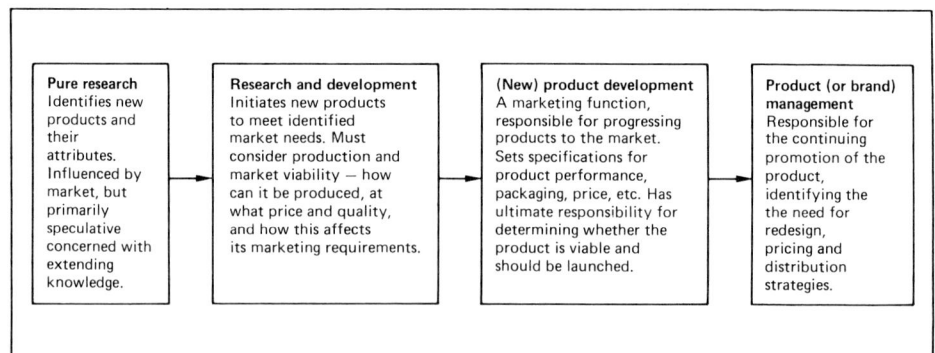

| **Pure research**
Identifies new products and their attributes. Influenced by market, but primarily speculative concerned with extending knowledge. | **Research and development**
Initiates new products to meet identified market needs. Must consider production and market viability – how can it be produced, at what price and quality, and how this affects its marketing requirements. | **(New) product development**
A marketing function, responsible for progressing products to the market. Sets specifications for product performance, packaging, price, etc. Has ultimate responsibility for determining whether the product is viable and should be launched. | **Product (or brand) management**
Responsible for the continuing promotion of the product, identifying the the need for redesign, pricing and distribution strategies. |

Figure 38 The product development process

●●

CASE STUDY: Salter Housewares Ltd

In the early seventies the company was approached by a Swiss designer with his design for a new concept in kitchen scales, which was ultimately launched as the Weighmix. The unique design features were the use of a mixing bowl as the scale's scoop, in which food was weighed (hence the name), and the ability to re-zero the scale so that ingredients could be added to the bowl one at a time and did not need to be transferred to another bowl.

The company was part of a medium-sized private group and was able to set up a task force of managers to progress the product to launch. This comprised the Production Manager and Research Engineer to carry out the R&D work, while the Marketing Director and a Product Manager were responsible for the product development phase. They commissioned the packaging and promotion materials, prepared forecasts of sales and prices, and briefed the sales force and major customers.

After its launch the Product Manager added Weighmix to his normal responsibilities for that part of the company's product range.

●●

Market research and product development

The development of the new product, once the basic concept exists, usually involves some market research.

ACTIVITY

86

➤←

2 mins

If you were responsible for market research in the development stage of a new product, which research designs would you see as particularly appropriate? Check back to page 58 if you want to refresh your memory about the different research designs.

As we saw in the last chapter, market research can encompass a whole range of approaches. Testing new products often relies on respondents being able to try out the product. The use of hall tests is often the most appropriate method, particularly when other parts of the marketing mix, as well as the product are being tested.

Consumer panels are also used for new product testing, particularly when family or child responses are needed. This method also enables consumption to be researched over a period of time.

Qualitative research, using in-depth group discussions, is frequently employed, often in conjunction with the other forms of testing mentioned above. People's underlying feelings about a product, attitudes to its design, presentation, packaging, name or price can all be investigated in this way.

The case study on International Distillers and Vintners' (IDV) approach to product development illustrates this process well. In the market for alcoholic drinks the packaging is often as important as the contents in stimulating initial purchase. For this reason IDV test both independently, before fully testing them in the 'pseudo-purchase' hall tests described in the case study.

Test markets

The launch of a new product is a hazardous process. The uncertainty of its success, coupled with the high levels of investment involved, ensure there is a lot of risk attached to product development. Whether you are starting up in business in a small local market or working for a major multinational, the problems are basically the same, even if the scale is different.

To reduce the risks associated with a new product launch, it makes sense to try out the product in a small part of the market first. This is the process known as test marketing.

● ●

CASE STUDY: International Distillers and Vintners (IDV)

As the United Kingdom market for alcoholic beverages matures, so producers attempt to introduce more tightly targeted drinks. Because the companies involved are large ones, operating in large markets, a clearly defined strategy for new product development is important. At IDV a six-stage procedure is adopted for testing new products from concept to launch.

Stage 1 Initial concept
Qualitative research using small 'exploratory groups' of consumers are invited to discuss the initial product concept, suggesting improvements and discussing issues like name, label, bottle and complete packages (i.e. the various layers in the 'product onion'). About eight such groups would be involved, at first with few formal concepts to discuss, latterly with more developed samples in prototype bottles, labels etc.

Stage 2 Pseudo purchase test
A mock shop format is used, with comparable existing products in the same price range presented. Respondents are asked to indicate what their purchase choice would be. First second and third choices are recorded and expectations of taste identified. About ten to fifteen products would be offered to choose from, reflecting the highly fragmented nature of this market where few have products having a large market share. Around 500 respondents would be involved, using only the packaging in gauging their preferences.

Stage 3 Hall test for liquid

The hall test takes place in parallel to the pseudo-purchase test. Respondents undertake blind tastings of the product and comparable, successful, standard products. Five-point rating scales for quality, flavour, etc., are used, with a sample of between 50 and 100 respondents.

Scale 4 Placement
Continuing the blind tasting, respondents in the hall test are recruited to participate in a placement trial. This group take the paired but unidentified samples home and test them there on the whole household. Similar questionnaires to those used in the hall test are self-administered after this comparative testing.

Stage 5 Repeat purchase test (the total concept)
A new panel is recruited and respondents interviewed on initial reactions, including tastings, to the complete product (contents and packaging), tested, and questionnaires completed. The respondents are offered the opportunity to purchase the product at a discount, to test likelihood of repeat purchasing.

Stage 6 Test market
Only now would the complete, final product be launched in a test market. The complete process described here is illustrated in Figure 39 – the end product being the *screen*, or the final decision on the test launch. All available research evidence must now be evaluated, and a management decision taken about whether or not to go into full production.

● ●

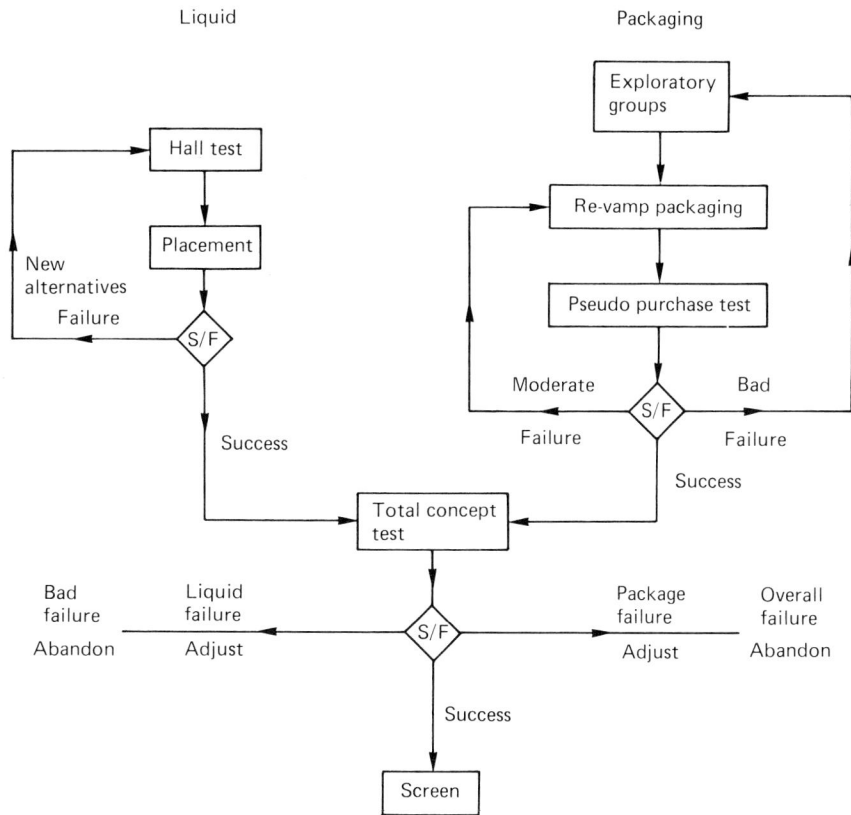

Figure 39 The IDV product screening process

A test market is defined by two things. It is limited in

- the length of time during which the product is offered to the test market;
- the range of possible customers to whom the product is available.

ACTIVITY

87

➔❬

2 mins

Why do you think these two limitations are placed on a test market?

The two limitations are important since the aim of the test market is to make a decision as to whether or not the product should go to a full launch. This is the decision as to whether it is a success or failure. The time when this decision is going to be made should be fixed before the test market starts to avoid temptations to 'wait a bit longer'.

By limiting the customer base you will be able to get some idea of what success you can expect to achieve. You will know the level of market penetration (proportion of the total market buying the product) you expect

115

to achieve. Success of the test market can then be measured in terms of whether or not this target has actually been reached.

If the product is to be supported by television advertising then an ITV television area will be the logical choice for a test market. It is possible to choose any of the areas available, but the cost will be lowest in a smaller area, particularly one with a concentrated population to make distribution easier. The ITV areas and the size of each area, in terms of households, are shown in Figure 40.

ITV Area	Contractor	Home ITV Households	
		'000	%
London	Thames TV (Mon–Thurs) LWT (Fri–Sun)	}4,323	21.0
Midlands	Central Ind. TV	3,374	16.4
North West	Granada TV	2,516	12.2
Yorkshire	Yorkshire TV	2,227	10.8
Cent. Scotland	Scottish TV	1,263	6.1
Wales & West	HTV	1,741	8.5
South & S. East	TVS	2,003	9.7
North East	Tyne Tees TV	1,144	5.6
East	Anglia TV	1,521	7.4
South West	TSW	610	3.0*
N. Ireland	Ulster TV	465	2.3
Border	Border TV	246	1.2
N. Scotland	Grampian TV	442	2.1
All ITV Areas		21,875 (Gross)	106.2**

*Including the Channel Islands.
**Reflects overlapping reception areas.

Figure 40 ITV areas and audiences

The area covered by Tyne Tees is a favourite test market, having 1.1m households, most of them in the two clusters around Tyneside and Teesside. Both these conurbations also have their own independent radio stations (Metro Radio and Radio Tees) and seven local daily morning or evening newspapers, plus a local Sunday paper.

This well-defined market, with a variety of local media, makes an ideal area to test new products. The use of merchandisers to assist in achieving speedy penetration of the distribution system is explained in Book 3. In essence, the objective is to get as many products on display as quickly as possible, to coincide with the appearance of the advertising.

Why do you think it is so important to get goods on display at exactly the same time as the promotion campaign starts?

If you think about it there are only two other possibilities; the product is available after the promotion starts, or before it!

Not being able to supply once demand is stimulated is the worst possible option; the effort put into getting people interested is being wasted, and the lack of a product may have the negative effect of producing dissatisfaction and disappointment.

If making customers wait is bad, surely having products available before launch is a good thing? Although there may be good reasons for pre-launch sales and deliveries they do have the effect of dissipating the launch campaign.

However, pre-launch sales or deliveries can be a useful way of favouring special customers, or overcoming the possible problems of coping with an initial surge of demand. They can also help to test the organisation's ability to supply – a pre-test before the test market!

Having identified the test market geographically, and determined when the launch is planned to start, you must also decide when it is due to end.

A number of decisions will need to be made about the product and its marketing towards the end of the test market. Can you identify two or three of them?

Compare your answers with the ones on page 138.

The level of promotion possible for the launch of a new product is higher than will be normal during its life, and the length of time for which this expensive activity can be sustained is limited. An adequate level of sales to operate profitably with a full launch must be achieved during this period or the decision must be made to stop now.

The launch decision

The decision not to go ahead with a full launch, and kill off a new product in its infancy is the hardest one to make. Whatever the product is – a good or a service – a lot of money will already have been spent on it. This 'sunk capital' cannot be unspent, so the temptation may be to try a bit longer and see if things pick-up, generating a bit more income to justify all that initial expenditure. At this point, it is important to consider some of the financial implications of marketing.

One of the most important practical considerations associated with the introduction of a new product is 'cash flow'. The graph in Figure 41 illustrates the idea. All the cash generation in the months before launch is negative, i.e. the company is spending money on the product without earning anything from it. Obviously that can't go on for ever.

For the product illustrated in Figure 41, the organisation's revenue equals its expenditure (known as 'breaking even'), in the eighth month after launch. However, the product is only breaking even on a month-to-month basis. What it hasn't done is to reduce the enormous backlog of expenditure it built up in the first seventeen months of development! This type of financial data applies whether the organisation is profit or non-profit making.

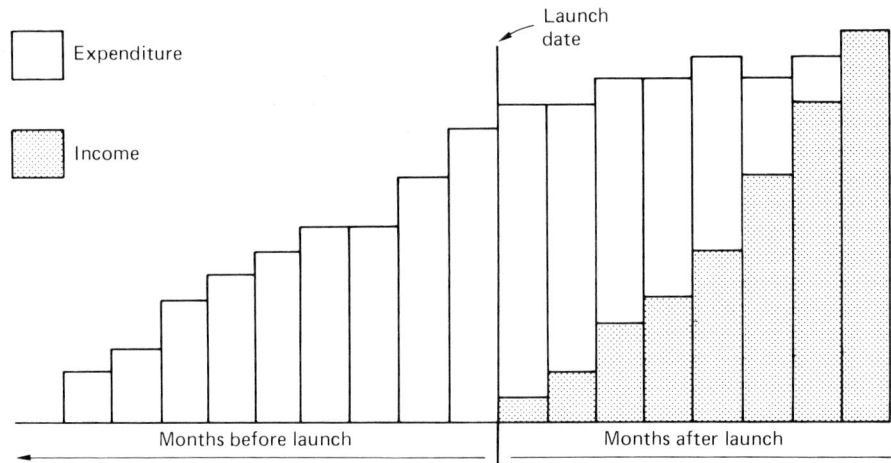

Figure 41 Income and expenditure for a new product

When monthly revenue equals expenditure then the net outflow of funds stops; the product now has to make some sort of surplus to regain that accumulated outflow before it is even in a position to consider whether or not it should be making a profit.

You can imagine that if sales failed to pick up so that the break-even point was not reached during the initial introduction, that downward curve showing the net outflow of money would just keep on falling. This is the reason many new firms fail; even if they are approaching break-even on their weekly or monthly sales. They have just run out of money because of the accumulated outflow; accountants call this a negative cash flow – for the people concerned it's called disaster!

You will now begin to appreciate the significance of the test market. If it tells you that there's no real market for the product at the price needed to achieve break-even, then the extra costs, and losses, of a full launch can be avoided.

For a public sector organisation, where revenue may not be linked to take-up (because customers don't pay for the service when they use it, like health care for example), this principle still applies. There may not be a financial break-even, but there is still a need to establish a minimum level of demand to justify the launch of the new product. Setting such targets may also include measures of 'quality' of provision as well as 'quantity'. Clearly the measurement of quality is not easy, nor is it easy to say how high a level of performance justifies any expenditure. Nevertheless, in establishing the market potential of a new product, you must have some idea of what level of demand justifies spending money on provision. If the market is large enough to ensure adequate uptake, the product's development becomes justified.

ACTIVITY

90

5 mins

A polytechnic has decided to launch a new course in Marketing. The Academic Board (the polytechnic's decision-making group) has said that the course must recruit forty students a year to justify setting it up. However the team developing the course has two years to reach this level of intake. The course will recruit nationally and, for the first year, it has been decided to aim to attract 20 students, to test the market, and the college's ability to deliver a high quality course.

In practice only 16 students are recruited, two of whom are mature students with work experience for whom the agreed entry requirements, normally 2 A-levels, are relaxed. As Polytechnic Marketing Officer what advice would you give to the course team and the Academic Board?

Write a very brief memo setting out your thoughts.

Compare your answer with the one on page 138.

Managing a product portfolio

A product portfolio is something like a pack of cards. Imagine a player with a hand of cards all from one suit, held up like a fan. Each card is different, yet they all fit together, thirteen hearts, or diamonds, etc.

A product portfolio shares many of these characteristics. It is a range of products which complement each other and fit together logically. In this section we will look at the idea of the product portfolio, how it can be analysed, and its product development implications.

In practice, there are many single product organisations, relying on selling into a single market for their continued existence. Such a position will always make them vulnerable.

The organisation relying on a single product in a single market will always have to fear a change in the pattern of demand; since it has nothing else to offer the market, or any other market, it has nothing to switch its production and marketing efforts to if consumer tastes change.

A company like this is also vulnerable to competition; a new entrant to the market will, unless it increases total market size, reduce the market share of existing participants. The nature of the market for some products may also be vulnerable to changes made by the government in regulations affecting suppliers or in taxes and duties.

The single product/single market company doesn't have the 'cushion' of other products and markets to support it. On the other hand, an organisation which puts its efforts into a host of different markets, with a range of unrelated products avoids this problem. What it has instead is the problem of managing such a range coherently.

The problem of managing a range of products coherently

The dissipation of effort may make it increasingly difficult to make the right decisions, as senior managers lack a clear insight into the marketing and production issues facing them.

ACTIVITY

91

3–5 mins

Figure 42 shows the four typical combinations of market and product range. Can you think of examples of organisations which fit reasonably well into each of the boxes A, B, C and D?

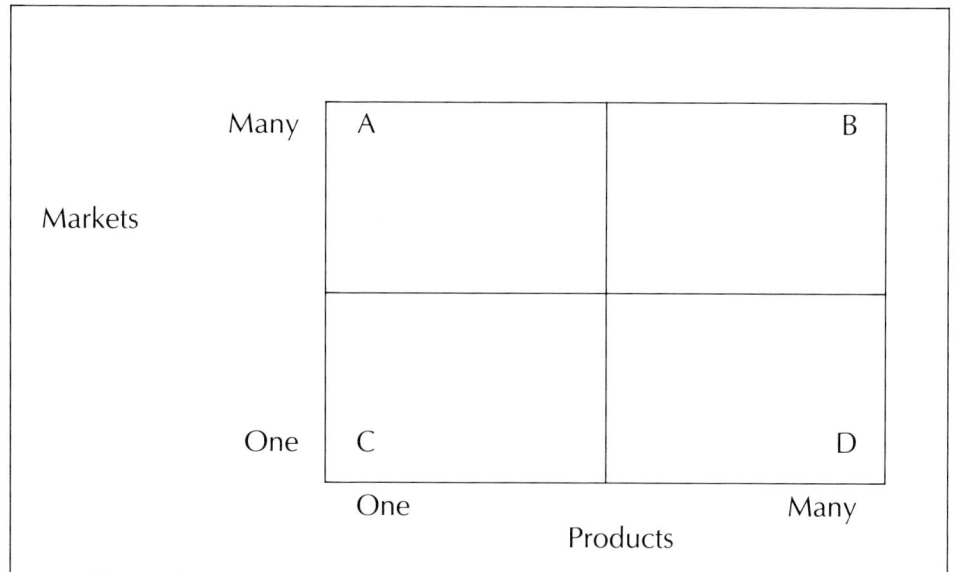

Many | A | B

Markets

One | C | D

One | Many
Products

Figure 42 The market/product mix

Compare your ideas with the ones we have provided on page 139.

The development of a product portfolio reflects both the organisation's need to create long-term stability by spreading its risks, and the changes that occur in the market-place. Of course, these two factors are interdependent; the changes which occur in the market place create much of the instability arising from rapid sales decline, as products reach the end of their life.

Building on a single product by the addition of complementary products leads naturally to a product portfolio. Further development into new market areas can be built into this strategy. It makes sense to approach these alternative developments (product and market) separately to avoid confusion; this approach also ensures that marketing resources aren't spread too thinly.

CASE STUDY: International Distillers and Vintners (IDV)

Whilst some products appear to be immortal – Mars bar, Cadbury's Dairy Milk – others will be replaced in the market's affections over time. It was the threat of changes in the market to its traditional products that prompted IDV to take a deliberate decision to expand from its traditional base as a wine importer and bottler and (Gilbey's) gin distiller, into new and complementary products.

The development of a successful portfolio of products requires patience; the company recognises that its failure rate in new products – those that fail to achieve long-term market position – can reach 80%! Nevertheless in a thirty-five year period IDV has added to its portfolio:

1953	Smirnoff vodka (top UK brand by 1980)
1966	Croft sherry (number 1 in Scotland and number 2 in the UK 1981–6)
1975	Baileys Liqueur (world number 2 1986)
1976	Piat d'Or branded table wine (UK number 4 1986)
1979	Malibu Liqueur (UK number 3 1986)

One interesting feature of the portfolio expansion is the rate of new product development which is continuing to increase, as more and more new products are launched in response to rapidly changing market tastes.

Developing a new portfolio and managing an existing one require slightly different approaches. It can be easy to ignore the fact that a portfolio of products is not fixed – each product is likely to be at a slightly different stage in its product life cycle. Ideally most products will be at various points through their maturity phase, a few will be in decline, and a few will be in introduction and growth phase (to replace the declining products).

ACTIVITY

92

>←

5 mins

Taking those three categories 'introduction and growth', 'maturity' and 'decline'. What level of marketing expenditure do you think should be devoted to each of them:

- *an average level;*
- *an above average level;*
- *a below average level;*

Fill in the grid below by putting a cross (×) in the box to show your view of the right combination of marketing expenditure to be associated with the product's position on the life cycle.

		Marketing expenditure		
		Below average	Average	Above average
	Introduction and growth	☐	☐	☐
Life cycle position	Maturity	☐	☐	☐
	Decline	☐	☐	☐

Compare your answers with the ones on page 139.

In considering expenditure on promotion, the watchword should always be 'don't throw good money after bad'! If a product is in decline it should be allowed to die peacefully; the point of having new products is to replace old ones. The heaviest expenditure should be given to the new products, the lowest should be devoted to old ones.

Age alone is not the sole determinant of the life cycle. As we saw in the first Workbook in the series, some products go through all the stages of the product life cycle in a very short time, while others keep going for decades. Extension strategies (to relaunch products in their maturity phase) can help here.

Extension strategies can range from major product redesign to minor changes in the marketing mix. They are primarily intended to stimulate demand in existing markets or introduce a product into new markets.

ACTIVITY

93

>←

3 mins

Why might an organisation decide to extend the life of existing products, rather than bring in new ones?

Trying to extend the life of a dying product

Once a product has entered its decline phase, trying to extend its life is putting off the inevitable, often at great cost. But while a product is still in its maturity phase, with healthy sales, an extension strategy can maintain or increase that market performance at far less cost than introducing new products.

This is because an existing, mature product has a firm base, with established brand recognition and brand loyalty. New sales in the existing market or in new markets, can be achieved from this base. A new product lacks this recognition and loyalty and the greater cost and uncertainty attached to establishing these can make extending the life cycle of existing products a far more attractive proposition.

But is this always a worthwhile strategy for all mature products or brands? The answer is no. Deciding which products are worth additional marketing treatment is the function of *portfolio analysis*, because it forces us to look at a product's suitability from the viewpoint of the market; does the market justify any extra treatment?

There are a number of possible approaches to portfolio analysis, but the most widely known is the product screening approach developed by the Boston Consulting Group. The Boston or BCG Matrix is illustrated in Figure 43.

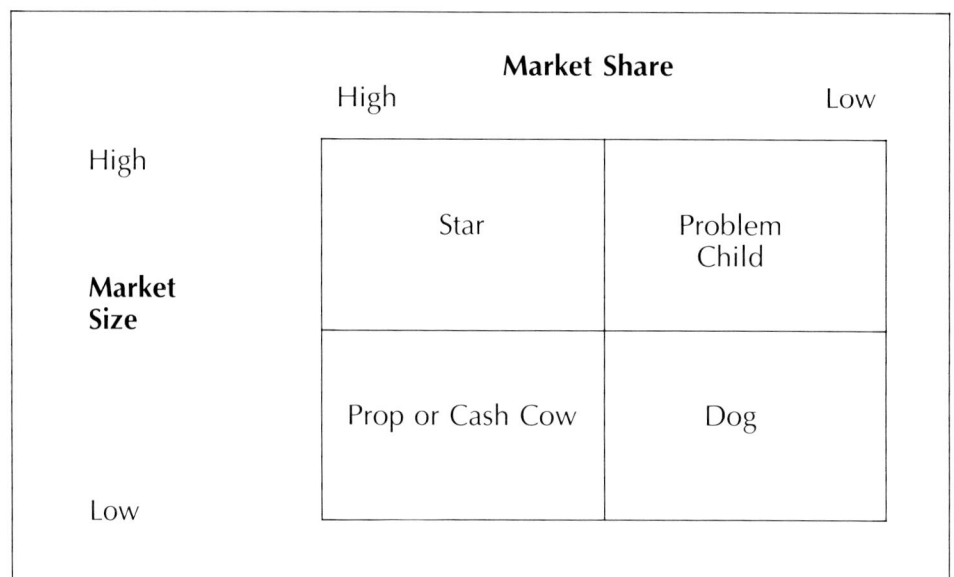

| | **Market Share** | |
	High	Low
High **Market Size**	Star	Problem Child
Low	Prop or Cash Cow	Dog

Figure 43 The Boston Matrix

The BCG approach is to classify products into one of four groups, Stars, Cash Cows, Problem Children and Dogs. The Stars are products which are dominant in large markets; they will be under a lot of attention from competitors, but they are the organisation's jewel in the crown. Products like Heinz Baked Beans, Mars Bars and Persil Automatic each dominate their respective markets. Props (or Cash Cows) support the organisation; they are likely to take proportionally less marketing expenditure than other products, and produce proportionally higher profits. An example is the Land Rover, which manages to dominate its particular market, a market which is a relative drop in the ocean compared with the total market for cars. (On the other hand, the Range Rover market represents a very different marketing scenario, a Star with intense competition from Japanese 'me-too' products!)

There is probably little potential for growth in market share for either, but Stars will have more potential than Props. They also have potential for *brand proliferation*; this means generating different versions of the product aimed at different market segments. This proliferation makes life harder for competitors and gives the organisation greater stability in the market, because it is now resting on two or more products rather than one. What's more, the chances of a higher total market share increase.

Good examples of brand proliferation exist in all three markets mentioned above; the baked bean market is part of the larger market which includes tinned spaghetti as well. Next time you visit the supermarket, look at the range of variants available in both parts of that market. For Mars the list of competitors include Milky Way, Twix, Kit Kat, Lion, Double Decker, etc. – most of these and the many other similar products come from only three manufacturers. Finally, while you are in the supermarket, look at the detergent shelves and consider that nearly all the detergents sold in Britain (including 'own brands') come from only three companies. That's brand proliferation!

The Problem Children are products which are underperforming; here extension strategies and product development may lead to growth in market share. They merit attention, which is more than can be said for Dogs! These are failing, and failing in unattractive markets. Even if sales are not declining there is a good case for withdrawing from that market if resources could be put to better use elsewhere.

One thing to stress here is that product divestment – withdrawing from the market – is a positive strategy if it's done to free resources for more attractive uses. It's a negative strategy if it's done as a last resort under market pressure. After all a product which is still selling, albeit not very well, might be attractive to another supplier.

This is why we talk about divestment rather than closure. There might be a competitor in the market who would happily take on your Dog, to join theirs and become a Cash Cow! What's more, they may be able to devote resources to the market to turn it into a more attractive proposition. With both of you in it, it's not worth doing but with one of you gone it becomes worthwhile.

You have seen how new products are developed from original concept to final launch, and some of the techniques available to reduce the risks associated with such launches. You have also seen that the lives of existing products can be extended to maximise the return they offer an organisation. Finally you have seen how the whole product range needs to be managed in the context of changing markets and the life of each product.

The final activity demonstrates a number of these issues; in tackling it you should look at how the ideas and techniques you have been introduced to might be used.

ACTIVITY

94

➤←

25 mins

During the seventies and eighties the major oil companies have rationalised their outlets, closing small petrol stations and opening large new ones in prime locations. These feature shops, car washes and even cash dispensers for banks as additional services. Yet throughout the country a number of small local distribution companies have been established, taking over the smaller outlets and operating them profitably.

Given this situation, try answering the following questions:
a) How did the small outlets in question fit into the oil 'majors' product portfolios?
b) Why did the small local companies find these outlets more attractive than the 'majors' did?
c) What are the attractions to oil companies of selling products other than petrol?
Write a few sentences to explain your answer to each question, then compare your ideas with the ones provided on page 140.

a)

b)

c)

THIRD PROGRESS TEST

Work through this final progress test, then check your answers on page 143.

1. Complete the following sentence:

   The .... product consists of the .... product with the addition of packaging, display material, the image of the distribution outlet, price and brand image.

2 List the four functions of packaging:

   a)
   b)
   c)
   d)

3 The three product development strategies listed each relates to new or existing products or market. For each one, indicate which by writing 'new' or 'existing' in the spaces provided.

Strategy	Product	Market
a) New product development		
b) Market development		
c) Diversification		

4 How do we describe a strategy based on copying other organisations' products?

5 How does 'pure' research differ from 'research and development'?

6 Which two features are used to limit a test market?

   a)

   b)

7 'Negative cash flow' means:

   a) an organisation is having to pay its suppliers;

   b) the money flowing into an organisation exceeds money flowing out;

   c) the money flowing out of an organisation exceeds money flowing in;

   d) investors are selling their shares.

Underline the correct answer.

8 Which of the following is most likely to be a candidate for product divestment? Underline the correct answer.

   a) a Star   c) a Problem Child
   b) a Prop   d) a Dog

Answers to Activities

ACTIVITY 7

The customers who go to Metrocentre come predominantly from the 'higher' social classes (ABC1); these three groups account for 53 per cent of customers although they only make up a fraction under 40 per cent of the population. This fits in with the high car usage and also reflects the low proportion of customers over 60, since many pensioners are in social class group E.

Knowing this, and the fact that far more women than men visit Metrocentre, the type of shops, the goods sold and even the toilet facilities can be designed to suit this customer profile.

ACTIVITY 8

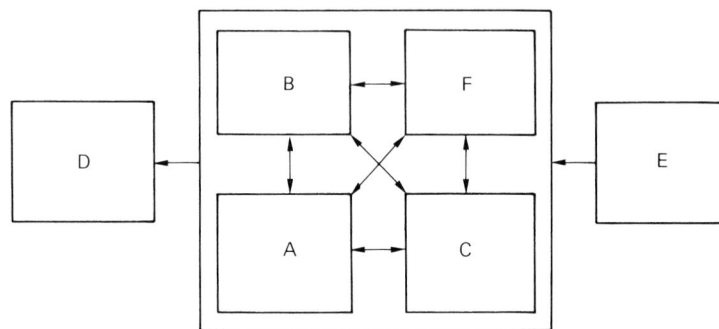

Figure 44

ACTIVITY 9

a) 60 visits
b) 30 orders
c) 60/5 = 12 visits per day
    30/5 = 6 orders per day
d) 60/30 = 2 visits to obtain one order
He is better than average.

ACTIVITY 11

Statements 1 and 2 are clearly straightforward quantitative information; statement 3 is qualitative, statement 4, although it appears to be descriptive in explaining why housewives bought the product is essentially quantitative data. It's a count of people answering a question in a particular way.

The final statement, although it came from six housewives, is qualitative data. It summarises their discussions rather than counting responses.

ACTIVITY 18

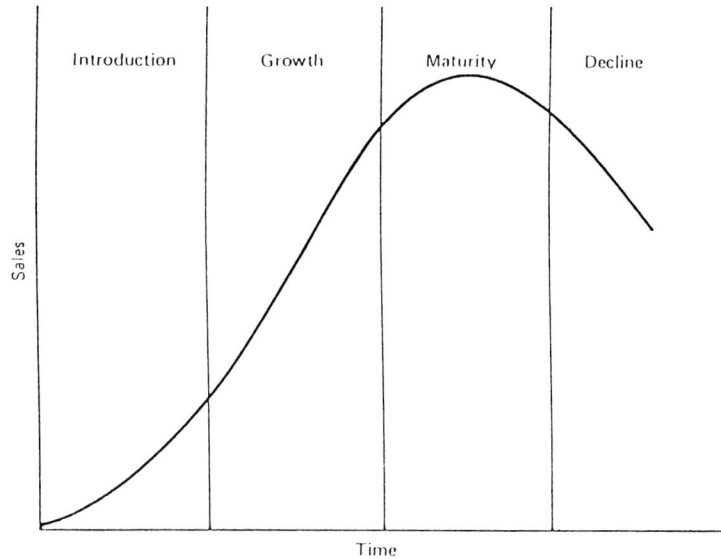

Figure 45

ACTIVITY 19

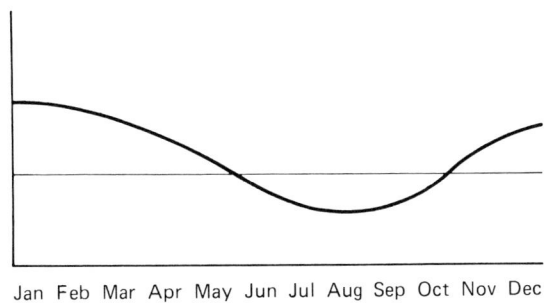

Jan Feb Mar Apr May Jun Jul Aug Sep Oct Nov Dec

Figure 46

Although electricity boards can't directly stimulate sales of electricity, they promote products which use electricity and which are not used for space heating, such as dishwashers and fridges. These will lead to a slightly more even pattern of demand.

ACTIVITY 20

The sales figures show a regular seasonal cycle which peaks during the summer, when gardening is at its height, and declines towards the end of the year. Ladies boots and coal would tend to do the reverse in the winter months, whilst dog food and hand cream are unlikely to have any marked seasonal fluctuation.

ACTIVITY 21

The decision by a competitor to undertake a new advertising or promotion campaign, launch a new product range, or cut their prices could all undermine your predictions.

ACTIVITY 25

This example shows that it is important to distinguish between data-gathering and decision-making. Market information systems, whatever form they take, just provide information for marketing managers who have to assess the risks and make the final decisions.

ACTIVITY 27

The trick here is to take the total number of journeys for each purpose (from the ninth column) and multiply it by the appropriate percentage figure from the second column, to give you the actual number of journeys for each purpose.

> e.g. for the first 'Purpose of journey' in the table, 'To and from work', the calculation is as follows:

$$11\% \text{ of } 84\ 200 = \frac{11}{100} \times 84\ 200 = 9262$$

We have set out the answers to the calculations needed for this Activity in the table below.

Purpose of journey	% by bus	No. of journeys in sample	Actual number of journeys by bus
To and from work	11	84,200	9262
In course of work	1	11,900	119
Education	24	21,200	5088
Escort for work	0	8,000	0
Escort for education	3	8,300	249
Shopping	18	71,900	12,942
Personal business	10	46,400	4,640
Social/entertainment	9	97,000	8,730
Holidays etc	2	19,900	398
All purposes	11	368,800	40,568

The answers to the questions in Activity 27 are therefore:

a) 40 568 bus journeys in total were included in the survey.
b) Shopping (12 942 journeys) and going to work (9262 journeys) were the two most popular reasons for travelling by bus.

ACTIVITY 28

At the very least you will be able to find out how many other suppliers there are in your area, and where they are located. You will also have a list of the plumbers and heating contractors who are potential customers. This list could be used for direct mailing purposes. By checking entries under related headings (e.g. 'building supplies' or 'building contractors') you will know how many specialise, and how many offer a wider range of services.

You will also probably be able to find out which of the firms have only one base or outlet, and which operate from more than one address (and are therefore likely to be far bigger). You can also refer to directories for neighbouring areas to help extend this type of analysis.

ACTIVITY 29

The popularity of whisky amongst golf players is far greater than the other sports, with 13.10 per cent of golfers being 'heavy' drinkers, against an average of 7.36 per cent. In fact, the players of football (6.01 per cent), tennis (6.58 per cent) are less likely to drink whisky heavily than in the population generally. Therefore, to promote your brand to existing drinkers, you should go for golf. However if you want to convert consumers of other drinks then you could choose any of three 'below average' sports. The 'index' is the easiest way of picking out these facts since it compares each group with the average of all consumers. An index above 100 (like golfers at 178) shows above average consumption, whilst less than 100 is below average.

ACTIVITY 31

Report on the market for -----: years 1–5

The first year's sales for this product (from Figure 9) match the expected pattern of the product life cycle, as they grow from its introduction into its maturity phase. This pattern continues in years 2 and 3, and is forecast to continue into year 5. However, the total sales for the industry (from Table 4) suggest that the market is still expanding, leading to this product having a declining market share (from 27.3 per cent in year 2 to a forecast 22.5 per cent in year 5).

The evidence of retailer resistance suggests that a number of factors may be causing this failure; these include price, promotional strategies and delivery. Clearly a product which fails to match competitors' service standards will not be seen to justify its higher price.

74 per cent of orders are delivered outside the competitors' 48-hour time; 5 per cent are cancelled, possibly due to the late delivery. 5 per cent of the sales in year 5 is worth £1.1m, over 1 per cent of the total market!

It is in the firm's interest to improve its distribution system, while reconsidering promotional and pricing strategy. However it should not simply cut prices, as this may damage its long-term profitability.

ACTIVITY 33

You will have had no difficulty in identifying questions a) and c) as the best starting points for market research. Questions b) and d) are much too vague in their present form.

ACTIVITY 34

They would probably have wanted answers to the following questions:

a) What services do our patients expect to receive from the Health Centre?
b) How do they perceive the services they currently receive?
c) How accurately can they identify the services we offer?
d) What are the strengths/good features of the current service?
e) What are the weaknesses/bad features of the current service?

You may have thought of others. Think about why yours are not the same as ours – are they simply more specific, or have you identified other major areas on which information could be supplied?

ACTIVITY 36

A checklist of factors to be used in choosing a Market Research agency might include:

- Convenience – are they easily accessible for meetings?
- Experience – do they know your industry or firm or will they have to spend time (and money) learning about you?
- Past contact – have you (or any of your colleagues) had any previous experience of the agency? If so, was it good or bad?
- Efficiency – how well did they respond to any enquiries you have made?
- Personal relationships – how well do you get on with the research executive? (Remember, he or she may be in contact with you quite a lot!)
- Cost – how do their quotations match up to any other proposals you may have received? (Unless you have had plenty of previous experience you may need to have several firms put up proposals to help you decide.)
- Enthusiasm – how keen are they to have your business?
- MRS/IMRA membership – are the staff of the agency members of the professional body or otherwise qualified to offer such services?

ACTIVITY 37

The research executive's first advice would probably be along these lines:

This case study offers plenty of opportunity for desk research into the size of the two proposed markets, their compatibility in terms of product requirements, distribution outlets, and pricing, and promotional media. It might also make sense to approach such large new markets one at a time!

ACTIVITY 38

In a personal interview, the interviewer has greater control, more variety is possible in question design (e.g. using prompts) and it may be possible to achieve a more representative sample. These advantages have to be weighed against the lower cost and greater speed of response possible using telephone interviews.

ACTIVITY 39

There is no control over who answers the questionnaire (it could be a joint effort) or when they will do it (responses could be received long after the survey has been completed). It is also difficult to know how representative the return is. The topic of the questionnaire might have more appeal for a particular group – for example, teenaged girls, or old age pensioners, and so distort the data collected.

ACTIVITY 40

- By definition consumer panels are different from the population at large since they have agreed to participate in the panel.
- They may not always represent the population at which a product is being targeted (not the right age, sex, social class or geographical location).

- They might also be slower to provide the information required, as products have to be sent out to them for test, while a hall test can be mounted very quickly.

ACTIVITY 41

Most fmcg (fast moving consumer goods) rely on shelf-space for sales; the greater the display and the more prominent it is, the more that is likely to be sold. A comparison of two products' shelf-space and position is a good indicator of relative sales performance.

ACTIVITY 42

The research executive suspects the attention your product is attracting may not be altogether a good thing.

Group discussions reveal that participants think the packaging is too complicated, and doesn't indicate clearly enough what it contains. The fact that your packaging catches people's eyes does not mean they will buy the product. It is as important to know how they react to the product and its packaging. One of the great myths in marketing is that there is no such thing as bad publicity. Simply being known or noticed is not enough. The objective is to stimulate people into a positive response which means they must be able to understand the images created by packaging (and other publicity materials) as well as notice them.

ACTIVITY 45

This is to avoid respondents looking ahead at other questions or looking at confidential guidance to interviewers, information which might bias their response. If prompt cards are used, they can also vary the order of options to avoid biasing responses towards the top items in the list.

ACTIVITY 46

In each case a yes/no answer is possible but it doesn't necessarily give a clear picture of your attitudes and behaviour. Watching *News at Ten* once in your lifetime is not the same as every night, nor would people's attitudes to sentencing policies easily fit into the simple black and white categories suggested by the question. Better questions would be:

- Did you watch any part of *News at Ten* last night?
- Have you eaten Heinz Baked Beans any time in the last month?
- Do you think any adult convicted of a crime which involved physical violence to another person should always receive a prison sentence irrespective of the amount of injury caused?
- Did you read any part of a Sunday paper last Sunday?

ACTIVITY 48

'Foreign cars are more reliable than British cars.'

Option	(a) Value	(b) Respondents	(c) [(a)×(b)]
Strongly agree	+2	53	+106
Agree	+1	35	+35
Uncertain	0	7	0
Disagree	−1	4	−4
Strongly disagree	−2	1	−2

+ 135 − 100 = 1.35

This means that the average or typical score given by 100 respondents is 1.35.

Figure 47

+1.35 is stronger than 'agree', but not 'strongly agree'. This suggests that people tend to feel fairly strongly that foreign cars are more reliable than British cars.

ACTIVITY 49

If no neutral score exists respondents are forced to choose between the two choices, which prevents them taking the easy option and 'sitting on the fence' if they are having problems deciding. However, it can also lead some respondents not to answer at all, or it may force an individual who really is neutral to make a decision one way or the other, against his or her better judgement.

ACTIVITY 50

Scaling questions can be used in all those research designs employing questionnaires or interview schedules – the first five in the list in Figure 15.

ACTIVITY 51

A poorly-designed questionnaire might indicate to respondents what the questions are concerned with, and thus encourage them to answer in a way they think you want to hear (or they might deliberately try to deceive you). Alternatively, questions might appear so trivial that the respondent gets bored, or so complex that they find the questionnaire too daunting to complete.

ACTIVITY 52

Standard introductions are used to prevent the respondents' answers being biased by different introductions, and to prevent information being given which respondents are not intended to have.

ACTIVITY 53

You will almost certainly have identified the two factors used most regularly to classify respondents – age and sex. (There is an old joke in market research that in analysing replies to questions, 'respondents are usually broken down by age and sex'!) You might also have mentioned social class, employment, education, marital status, family size, housing type and tenancy, location, race, religion or political affiliation. This is not an exhaustive list but contains the most commonly used classifiers.

ACTIVITY 55

	JICNARS grades	R-G's classification
Primary school headteacher	B	II
Secretary	C1	III(N)
Motor vehicle mechanic	C2	III(M)
Bricklayer's mate	D	V

ACTIVITY 56

You may have said this reflects a traditional view of married life (an employed husband married to a housewife not in paid employment) and this is not wholly inaccurate. Even in double income families the husband usually earns the higher income, and this tends to set the lifestyle and social status of the family. JICNARS do also ask for the 'Chief Wage Earner' to look for any variation in this pattern, but it is rare to find it. However families are increasingly found with only a single (usually female) parent, or an unemployed husband, and in this case a woman's occupation may be a determining factor.

ACTIVITY 57

All three! The magazine publisher may be interested only in accountants, and not other professional or managerial staff. A sock manufacturer may be interested in the differences between sedentary and active occupations. Macmillan Education Ltd are likely to be interested in both the occupational and educational details of existing and potential users of open learning materials, like you.

ACTIVITY 58

The analysis suggests that residents of large conurbations (towns and cities) whether in the centre or, even more importantly, the suburbs, are the most common users. As residence moves towards smaller and more rural areas, so bus usage falls. (Of course, other factors may be involved. For example, there could be fewer bus services available in certain areas.)

ACTIVITY 62

You probably suggested the following factors – that the population is:

a) not resident in the area concerned;
b) has visited or is visiting the area;
c) for a holiday.

Your population could therefore be defined, for example, as 'All adults temporarily present in the Borough of Seathorpe at any time between June 6th and 13th 199X who are not working or seeking work there'.

ACTIVITY 63

None of these examples is a random sample since, in turn, they exclude residents of all but two roads, nine out of ten households, and all non-users of the car park on that day, no matter how the roads were chosen, or the decision to select the tenth household and the place to start, or that particular car park and day.

ACTIVITY 65

The higher the level of precision, the larger the sample required, and the higher the cost, so a 99 per cent level is more expensive. However it is worth noting that as a population gets larger, the sample size only needs to grow slightly to achieve the same statistical level of precision. A sample of 1160 out of a population of 50,000 would give as much precision as a sample of 1173 out of a 100,000 population.

ACTIVITY 67

The survey could include questions about:

- the amount teenagers spend on clothes;
- when and how often they buy clothes;
- where they buy clothes;
- the influences on their clothes-buying decisions (family, friends, magazines, etc.);
- attitudes to fashion, styles, retail outlets, etc.;
- brand recognition;
- advertising recall.

You might have included other items; a list such as this can be endless! These are just a few of the most obvious topics to consider.

ACTIVITY 68

66 per cent of all respondents chose 'hotel/pension etc.', but there was strong variation between age groups below 45 and those above. This shows clearly that this type of accommodation has a much stronger appeal for older holiday-makers. The reverse is true for self-catering accommodation; villas, flats, chalets/cabins/caravans and tents.

We can probably conclude that comfort and service are more attractive to older age groups, who are also more likely to have the disposable income needed to afford them.

ACTIVITY 69

The conclusion to be drawn from the figures in the table is that as the size of the workplace increases (as measured by the number of employees), so the number of such workplaces ('census units') first increases up to 5–10 employees. This is positive correlation. From the 11–24 employees group on, the number of workplaces decreases as the size of the firm increases – a negative correlation.

ACTIVITY 70

Option (c) would be the best one to target. The attraction of caravan holidays will be, at least in part, the low cost; a low-price car is obviously going to offer a similar advantage, particularly with an improved towing capacity.

This is going to be a disadvantage to the groups in (a) and (d), where image and appearance would be undermined. The company driver will most probably have a company car. This is most likely to be a UK made (or 'badged') car, as this is the standard policy of most fleet car users. Here again there is the question of image. A low-priced car might suggest that the company had fallen on hard times.

ACTIVITY 71

The following report covers the main points which you could have included:

'We have carried out some research on our brand to find out whether shoppers know it, and if so whether or not they think it is reliable.

'The results are partly encouraging, partly discouraging. After talking initially to some small groups of women, 2000 women across the country in towns and cities, suburbs and country areas were asked if they knew about us. Unfortunately far more remembered our competitors X and Y than us, and those who did remember us tended to be older and less well-off.

'However the good news is that those who know us think highly of us. We were rated as being far more reliable than either X or Y! Clearly our primary aim now is to tell more people about us and let everybody know about the quality of our brand.'

ACTIVITY 76

The positive images for a paper bag you may have come up with could include: personal service, choice, freshly made, homely, to describe the paper bag. The clear stiff, plastic wrapping might suggest: hygiene; freshness; cleanliness; care; protection. Negative images for the paper bag might include; unhygienic, unprofessional, low quality; and mass production, 'plastic contents', artificial, over-priced, for the plastic wrapping.

ACTIVITY 80

	Existing products	New products
Existing markets	Current position	Product development
New markets	Market development	Diversification

Figure 48

ACTIVITY 82

There is a substantial investment needed to develop new products from scratch; in high-tech and pharmaceutical industries this may involve many years and many millions of pounds. This is all high risk investment since no useful product may result, or the product which does emerge may not have an adequate market.

If there is a market, the cost of developing that market (by sales and promotional expenditure) may still not be justified by the returns it could provide.

ACTIVITY 83

There are many products you could have listed. Our suggestions would be Ariel Liquid and the similar products which have followed it onto the market, and boy/girl disposable nappies, pioneered by Pampers and now featured in most competing brands.

Amstrad have been a very successful 'me too' company in the consumer electronics field.

ACTIVITY 85

There are many possible questions which could be asked, but your list should at least include:

- What are people's attitudes to existing analgesics, and particularly their fears of side-effects, if any?
- How do people feel about inhaling an analgesic as opposed to swallowing tablets or capsules as is more usual?
- If people would inhale, what form should an inhaler take to encourage its use?

ACTIVITY 89

The aim of the test market is to decide whether or not the product will be successful. This is the primary decision; however there may be others that will need to be made:

- Does the product need any further development or redesign before going national?
- Does any other aspect of the marketing mix need changing (packaging, advertising, sales promotion and point of sales display, pricing, distribution)?
- What level of sales could be expected for a national launch? Is this enough? Can delivery match such demand?

ACTIVITY 90

Your memo probably looked something like this:

Memo
From: Marketing Officer
To: Marketing Course Team
    cc Secretary Academic Board

Subject: First intake to marketing degree

In simple numerical terms, this performance clearly was not a success; the target of 20 students has not been achieved. It is probably not sensible to scrap the course after one year, but the course team needs to review, as a matter of urgency, all the elements of its marketing mix, if there is to be any chance of reaching the target of 40 next year.

As only two of the 16 recruits are mature students (12.5%), might it be worthwhile exploring the possibility of a special marketing effort aimed at this group?

ACTIVITY 91

Here are some examples of organisations which might fit into each of the boxes (although as you can see from our comments, almost all of them could be debatable!). You have probably thought of completely different ones, but you should be able to compare both lists to get a feel for the different types of product portfolio.

A *Many markets, one product*
British Gas sells its primary product into many different markets, both domestic and industrial. Since privatisation, it has tried to use marketing more effectively to extend its range of products.

B *Many markets, many products*
Any of the major multinationals, such as ICI, Proctor and Gamble or Unilever come into this category. Most have reached this position of strength by diversifying from single products or markets.

C *One product, one market*
Your local ice cream van sells cold confectionery to the leisure market. As such, it is very vulnerable to changes in fashion, or the weather.

D *Many products, one market*
A large UK retailer, such as Marks and Spencer or John Lewis, would be an example of this, although since they have moved into France as well, this might be less true of M & S. Other examples might include the big mail order companies, such as Freemans.

ACTIVITY 92

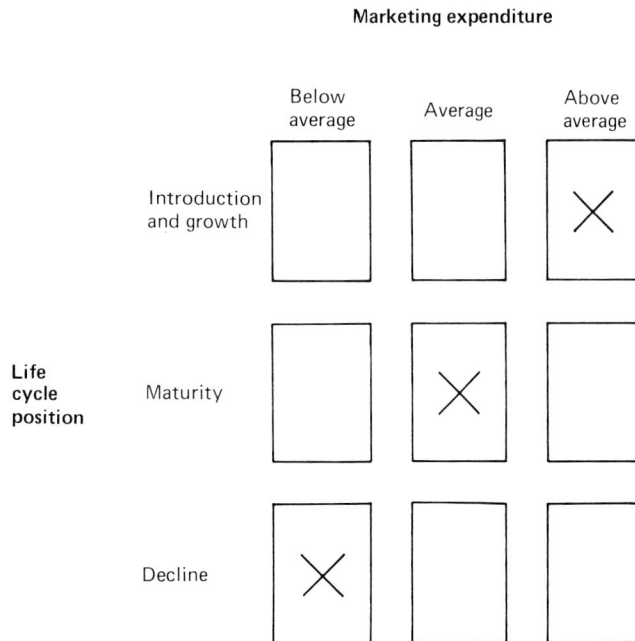

Figure 49

ACTIVITY 94

For the oil 'majors', the small outlets would, at best, be 'Props', having a high share of relatively small local market. Although they might be relatively profitable they would only manage low volumes compared with major outlets. The overheads from managing such outlets, however, would be the same as for the major outlets.

Furthermore, there would be little opportunity for growth in volume, due to limited size of the market, while in major outlets increased volume could be obtained as a result of new investment. On the other hand, for small distributors with low overheads geared up to supplying and managing small outlets, the ability to achieve a high market penetration of a market which for them is large, makes such outlets more like 'stars'.

The major oil companies see their future in augmenting the core product (petrol refining, distribution and retailing) by the high value-added services now obtainable at many of their retail outlets. Car washes, car-related products and spares, groceries, flowers and snacks can all generate additional income from customers stopping for fuel. The profit on these sales, which might only amount to a few pounds, will still be larger than that from selling a tank full of petrol.

What's more, the additional services augment the product in the customer's eye. He or she is not just stopping to buy fuel, but at a mini-shopping centre. Thus the availability of the services attracts customers to buy fuel, and customers who stop and buy fuel may be attracted to buy other goods.

In terms of the Ansoff Matrix, these companies are developing new products for existing customers, while at the same time hoping the new products will also attract new customers. For the small companies, the 'niche' operators, the takeover of small stations allows them to consolidate by keeping within an existing product area, and rely upon existing local customers to ensure a low risk expansion.

Answers to Progress Tests

First Progress Test

1 Market research is the process by which an organisation investigates its market (or potential market) to assess reaction to product, price, promotion and distribution.

   Score 1 mark if your sentence was along these lines.

2 The four parts of MIS are

   a) Marketing records
   b) Desk research
   c) Statistical and econometric models
   d) Commissioned market research

   Score 1 for each one correctly identified (maximum 4 points).

3 Statements a), c) and e) are examples of quantitative information.

   Score 1 for each one correctly identified (maximum 3 points).

4 An organisation's marketing records are based on existing information about the customer.

   Score 1 for correct answer.

5 The product life cycle is an example of a statistical model.
   Score 1 for correct answer.

A total of ten points was possible. If you scored 8 or more, move on to Chapter 3. If you scored less than this, you would probably benefit from reading through Chapter 2 again, and concentrating on any aspects you weren't sure about, before moving on.

Second Progress Test

1 The market, suppliers.

   Score 1 for a correct sentence.

2 a) Market Research Society, b) Industrial Market Research Association.

   Score 1/2 for each correctly identified.

3 Personal interviews, telephone interviews, postal questionnaires, hall tests, consumer panels, audits, observation, qualitative research.

   Score 1/2 point for each technique correctly identified (maximum 4 points).

4 Postal questionnaires

   Score 1 for correct answer.

5 Closed or open ended

   Score 1/2 for each correct answer.

6 Prompt cards

   Score 1 for correct answer.

7 A *supplementary question* to *encourage recall*.

   Score 2 if your answer contained both these elements.

8 a) Rank order scale
   b) Likert Scale

Score ½ for each correct answer.

9 Ordinal scale

Score 1 for correct answer.

10 a) It is a leading question, suggesting the answer to be given.
    b) It would introduce bias in the survey data.

Score 1 for each answer if along these lines.

11 Occupation

Score 1 for correct answer.

12 A   Upper middle class
    B   Middle class
    C1   Lower middle class
    C2   Skilled working class
    D   Working class
    E   Lowest level of subsistence

Score ½ for each correct definition (maximum 3 points)

13 a) C2   b) E

Score ½ point for each correct answer.

Score 1 point for a correct answer to each of the following questions:

14 geodemographic

15 lifestyle classifications

16 random

17 sampling frame

18 99%

19 systematic

20 stratified

21 cluster

22 purposive

23 omnibus

24 positively correlated

25 cross-tabulation

The total possible mark is 32. If you scored 25 or over you have done well – move on to Chapter 4. If you scored 15–25, we suggest you work through Chapter 3 again before moving on. If you scored fewer than 15 you may want to contact your tutor to discuss any problems.

Third Progress Test

1 augmented, core

   Score 1 for a correct sentence.

2 a) Protection
   b) Ease of handling
   c) Point-of-sale display
   d) Promotion (as a premium offer in its own right)

   Score ½ for each one correctly identified.

3 *Strategy*   *Product*   *Market*

   a) New product development   New   Existing
   b) Market development   Existing   New
   c) Diversification   New   New

Score ½ for each one correctly identified (maximum 3 points)

4 A 'me-too' strategy

   Score 1 for correct answer.

5 'Pure' research doesn't necessarily take account of either marketing or production requirements, whereas R&D specifically does.

   Score 1 for a sentence along these lines

6 a) Time
   b) Geographical area or a similar division of the total market.

   Score 1 for each correct answer.

7 c)

   Score 1 for correct answer.

8 d) a Dog

   Score 1 for correct answer.

The maximum score was 11. You did well if you scored 8 or more. If you scored less than this, re-read the chapter to make sure you understand the points you got wrong.